The Power of UNITY

Empowered Believers
Empower the Church

Kathy J. Smith

The Power of Unity

Empowered Believers Empower the Church

Kathy J. Smith

Copyright © 2019 by Kathy J. Smith

ISBN 978-1-61529-209-7

Published by Vision Publishing
P.O Box 1680
Ramona, CA 92065
760 789-4700
www.booksbyvision.org

Scriptures found within this volume are from the New American Standard unless otherwise noted.

I just finished reading Kathy's book on the Power of Unity. I just love the way Kathy writes. Her book and her writing are easy to read and easy to digest. Some books I read I get lost after every other paragraph. This book is practical as well, as it will provoke us to take a biblical look at how God intended unity to function in our lives and in the life of the church.

I felt like in reading this book, I was reading a handbook on how God desires us to work together to fulfill his divine purposes on earth. The challenge for all of us will be in asking the Lord how to implement these truths into our lives and into our churches. If we could truly grasp "the power of unity" we could turn the world upside down...

Pastor Brian Weeks/Brian Weeks Ministries
and Solomon's Porch
Rehoboth, MA

Kathy masterfully shares how the work, operation and ministry of The Father, Son and Holy Spirit with their varying gifts function in the believer's life as the Church. Practical, powerful and applicable, this book will help leaders and all God's people walk together in unity to fulfill Gods plans and purpose.

Kathy mentions the church is now in an Esther moment to intercede and disrupt the enemy's plans, I couldn't agree more. Read and study this book to discover your potential as a healthy, connected and functioning part of God's Family / Church and see the world changed!

Mark McElwee, Pastor/ Senior Leader, Heart of God Church,
San Diego, CA

Unity in the Body of Christ was on the heart of Jesus as demonstrated in his high priestly prayer in John 17. In Christ, all have Holy Spirit, and in that sense, we are already one...but living it out is easier said than done. Dr. Smith is passionate to see the church working for the expansion of the Kingdom of God...submitted to the King and working together within locality. This book will challenge the reader to seek unity with purpose.

Stan E. DeKoven, Ph.D., MFT
Founder and President
Vision International University
Ramona, CA

The Power of Unity is a book that every team member, leader, and minister must read. This comprehensive guide provides the sought-after biblical principles and practical wisdom needed to effectively empower the church. It answers questions such as what is the purpose and responsibility of five-fold ministry? How do I cast the vision? And what do I do when I'm offended?

In a world where the church is under constant pressure to conform to humanistic beliefs that oppose the Word of God, The Power of Unity is a resource and a reminder that God has fully empowered His church to advance the kingdom, as we remain united in Him.

Dr. Cathy Guerrero
Regency Christian International Center
Whittier, CA

Table of Contents

Acknowledgments

I want to thank all who have helped complete this work with your input, encouragement, and prayers. My life group, the prayer team, my family and co-workers; there are too many to name individually but you know who you are.

Also, thank you to those who took time to preview the book and wrote recommendations. Thank you to Marti for your expertise in formatting.

Thanks to Dr. Stan DeKoven for editing, invaluable expertise and input, and encouragement. Thanks to Erma Kummerer for proofreading, support, and encouragement. Thanks to my pastor, Bob Roberts for his valuable input, encouragement, and for writing the foreword.

Thanks to you all, and to the Lord.

May God reward each one with his rich blessings and favor.

Sincerely,
Kathy

Foreword

Like most Pastors, I have earnestly prayed that God would grant me wisdom to establish a healthy spiritual environment within the church I pastor. This desire has sent me to countless seminars, and at times, it has made me vulnerable to the promises of empty prophets.

Over the years, I purchased kits, read books, and downloaded programs all promising they have the answer to church growth. Many of these promises failed to produce. As the book of Jude says, they were clouds without rain. I remember commenting to a fellow pastor, "There must be a better way."

That better way became clear when I had the privilege of reading a book by Dr. Kathy Smith titled, The Power Of Unity.

This book is not a shortcut to revival, but it reveals God's pathway for revival. God's pathway for a healthy environment that leads to true revival is found in the power of unity. But what are the markers of unity? How does one become united with community without sacrificing individuality? These and any manner of questions are addressed in this book. This is a must-read book for those who are serious about partnering with God to ensure the church can be all she was called to be. The Power of Unity should be on every Pastor's desk.

Pastor Bob Roberts
Senior Pastor – New Life Christian Fellowship
Grand Blanc, Michigan, USA

Introduction

In nearly thirty years of ministry, I have been honored to travel internationally to several different countries. Each time, I found myself touched by the outpouring of love by the people I was sent to serve. My most recent trip to Brazil was all that and more; to borrow a favorite phrase of a close friend, it was all that **AND** a bag of chips!

The hunger of the Brazilian people for God's word, and their reaction to the message, was like nothing I have ever witnessed before. Even in advance of my arrival the expectation of the people was high.

They prayed and prepared trusting God would move mightily; such expectation does not go unnoticed with God. I am reminded of the woman with the issue of blood, she expected and so she received. God honors faith and our heartfelt sense of expectation.

In the US, we are blessed with abundance. This includes an abundance of opportunities to hear and be taught the Word. It is however a double-edged sword. We have access to a wealth of knowledge via online learning, books, and television.

There are numerous church services, workshops and conferences where Christians gather to hear godly leaders preach, teach, and worship. We are a very blessed nation. Because this knowledge is readily available to us, we can mistakenly take it for granted.

The word that was shared began a stirring among the Brazilian congregation. They became excited, wanting to hear more and more. At first, I was bewildered by their reaction; I did not understand why they were so excited! Later Pastor Lucas explained that the preaching and teachings were fresh revelation to the people in Feira De Santana, Brazil.

Knowledge that had become common to me, was fresh revelation to them. They were stirred to act and respond to the word of the

Lord. They discussed it on their social media sites and called to speak with their pastors. They wanted to know more; more on how to develop healthy relationships with one another and how to fulfill their personal role in the body of Christ. They grasped the importance of each individual doing his part to change their church, their city, and their nation.

God is so good. Change does not begin by changing the masses, it begins with change in the one, ourselves.... and it trickles over to others. If we take responsibility for our own transformation, we can empower the church and expand God's kingdom on the earth.

The people of Brazil are fertile soil, and the word of the Lord is seed ripe with possibilities. I fully believe that God is preparing a bountiful harvest and a changed Brazilian nation. I hope you will join me and the thousands of others in praying for these beautiful people. God is up to something good.

Furthermore, let us pray for our own nation. May we awaken again to the excitement of hearing, receiving and acting on the word of the Lord. As previously noted, we are a nation that is rich with a wealth of knowledge. It is available at our very fingertips. Christian education opportunities are numerous.

If expectation and faith are the catalysts to change, let us prime the pump to receive. Change in our nation will not begin with the masses, it will begin with the one. Lord change me, that the blessings might flow. Lord bless this nation and start with me! Amen.

What Next?

Is it any wonder that people worldwide lay awake at night wondering what may come next? In a world that seems to be turned upside down and without faith, unity, even unity within the church, seems to be fleeting. Neighbor rises against neighbor, and family members are unable to agree; the idea of unity in the world as we know it seems nearly impossible.

The concept of free speech is challenged by those who feel they know what is best for all. Any who disagree with their personal ideology may find themselves the subject of angry outbursts, and at times, even violence. Actually, violent outbursts may be observed on all sides of the political spectrum. It would seem in some circles that freedom of speech only applies to those who comply with the concepts they mutually agree on.

Unity, ah yes. How might a city, country, nation, or even the church hope to achieve unity in a world so torn apart by controversy, violence, and hate? It can't, except by the grace of God. But for God, we would have no hope. But therein comes our peace and joy, that by His grace we will someday attain the unity that He himself has prescribed.

Unity is a healing prescription for disunity, and love is the remedy for hate. The church is the vehicle through which unity is to be delivered to the world. As Paul wrote in 1 Corinthians 15:55, *"Where, O death is your victory? Where, O death is your sting?"* Death, you seek to destroy us, but for God.

It is through the struggle for unity that the church will find its backbone, spread its wings, and become the light of the world; fulfilling the mandate of God as the bearer of peace and declaring the good news, the redemption from sin and eternal life.

For we know that the whole creation groans and suffers the pains of childbirth together until now. And not only this, but also, we ourselves, having the first fruits of the Spirit, even we ourselves groan within ourselves, waiting eagerly for our adoption as sons, the redemption of our body. Romans 8:22-23

The Struggle

Even the eagle knows not to fight the storm. The process of climbing higher allows it to soar above the tumultuous wind and the pounding rain. We cannot allow apprehension, anger, resentment, offense, fear, hate, or bitterness to overcome us when the day of trouble comes.

Emotional baggage weighs down our hope and hinders our movement. Its heaviness hinders our spiritual ascent. Rather, we must rejoice in the victory and promotion that are sure to come. We must rest in him and move forward in him, with the understanding that the storm is just a part of the process.

We know a caterpillar remains alone in the cocoon while it develops and transforms. These days are spent in sheer isolation. They are days of perfecting, growing, and becoming. Should the days in the cocoon be prematurely interrupted, the new butterfly will be too weak to survive. It is through the struggle to break free that the butterfly becomes strong; enabling it to spread its wings and fly. Independence and strength come as a result of the struggle.

The preparation and transformation process is well illustrated in the book of Esther. A season of perfecting was required before she could make her debut in the presence of the king. Esther submitted herself to the process.

God gave her favor with those who could advise, prepare, and provide for her all that she would need. Because she was submitted and obedient, she became an instrument of peace; and because she was faithful, she became the influential wife of the king. She is credited with delivering the Jews from certain death. I would submit to you that this is exactly where the church stands now.

In a world seemingly destined to destroy itself, there stands one sent by God to intercede and disrupt the enemy's plan. Even now, she is in her season of perfecting. She is the bride of Christ, the church. Anger, hatred, and disunity would tear us apart without remedy; but for God.

God says, we are salt and light. God says, we are the light of the world. God says, we are a city set on a hill that cannot be hidden (Matthew 5:14-16). But for God, there would be no remedy to the world's destruction. But in God, we are members of the body of Christ. We are the answer the whole world is seeking. Yes, we are the body of Christ; and He is the way, the truth, and the life. Church, we must arise and take our place! But truly, we cannot do so without unity.

Chapter One:

God's Plan

So, what is God's plan? I heard the Lord speak in my spirit, "Empower the individual believer and they will empower the church." Mature and healthy individuals fuel the effort of the collective body to come into unity. One mind, one spirit, and one body; unity enables and empowers the church to fulfill her role in history. Where do we begin? Change does not originate in the masses; it originates in the one.

God created man to be fruitful, multiply, tend the garden; and more importantly to have a close personal relationship with him. God wanted a family, so He created man in His own image, in their image (Godhead), and placed him in the garden where He could walk and talk with him. He was their father, and they were His children. They were to have dominion over all his creation, except for each other.

He placed them in paradise, the garden of Eden. Then the unthinkable happened; because of sin the relationship between God and man was interrupted. Being the loving father that He is, He had a plan to rescue man from his sin. Therefore, God's only begotten son, Jesus, shows up on the scene to rescue you and me.

He lived on earth for thirty years and began His ministry with a rag tag group of men that became His first twelve disciples. For three years He walked with them, He talked with them, He broke bread with them, and He showed them the Father. He planted the seed of the word in their hearts and demonstrated the manifestation of God's love through the many signs, wonders, and the miracles He performed.

Jesus envisioned the church, His body, as whole. He envisioned His body as unified, and so He prayed.

The glory which You have given Me I have given to them, that they may be one, just as We are one; I in them and You in Me, that they may be perfected in unity, so that the world may know that You sent Me, and loved them, even as You have loved Me. John 17:22-23

Jesus prayed that we would all be one. But how? How can people from so many different cultures, social backgrounds, walks of life, even different skin colors become one? It all begins with a relationship with Jesus.

We know that the first twelve disciples were a very unlikely group including fishermen, tax collectors, and a political zealot. Yet they all had one thing in common, their relationship with Jesus.

Relationships

I was recently contemplating the focus of this book. I knew that the topic was empowering the church through unity, but I wanted to hone the specifics of what God wanted me to share.

As I sat drinking my morning coffee, I asked God to clarify His message more fully. I heard, "Success and happiness are found in healthy relationships. The key is knowing those to keep, those to create, and those to walk away from." My takeaway from this is simple. Who you associate with and how is important! Developing healthy relationships is crucial.

It is not about who you are or where you come from, it is about who you know. The twelve disciples had this one thing in common, their relationship with the Lord.

They did not become seasoned apostles overnight, not by any stretch of the imagination. Instead, they began by sitting at His feet…learning, observing, and becoming.

Transformation is a process. It is a process that requires our co-operation.

And do not be conformed to this world, but be transformed by the renewing of your mind, so that you may prove what the will of God is, that which is good and acceptable and perfect. Romans 12:2

The twelve spent three years being discipled as followers of Jesus. Their relationship with one another, and with Jesus grew and matured. They learned to exercise their faith when Jesus sent them by twos to minister to the people. They experienced the many miracles that Jesus performed because they were there at His side.

They were also active participants in many of the ministry opportunities, such as feeding the crowds that had come to hear Jesus. Being with Jesus afforded them the luxury of hands on training. Their teacher did not just tell them what to do, He showed them. They had firsthand knowledge of all that He said and did. - This was possible because of the relationships they had developed.

Because of the relationship they had with Jesus, they became devoted and dedicated to serving him. As a result of the things that He taught, their minds were renewed. This rag tag group was transformed into the foundational leadership of the future church. Only God can transform a heart, but we must participate.

So then you are no longer strangers and aliens, but you are fellow citizens with the saints, and are of God's household, having been built on the foundation of the apostles and prophets, Christ Jesus Himself being the corner stone, Ephesians 2:19-20

Spiritual Maturity

We know that the disciples came together in the upper room on the day of Pentecost; it says they were all in one accord. They were able to come together as one through the commonality of the things they had both seen and experienced while Jesus mentored them.

They also had the same up close and personal relationship with Jesus. Some were closer than others, as John often reminds us in his writings; he was the disciple Jesus loved. However, they all spent three years of their lives with Jesus. They walked with him, talked with him, and did life together with him.

Unity Through Maturity

No longer were they spiritual children. They had grown in their knowledge of the word and through the exercising of their spiritual senses. Their relationship with Jesus had matured them. Spiritual maturity makes unity possible. It also opens the door to opportunity.

Paul writes:

> *until we all attain to the unity of the faith, and of the knowledge of the Son of God, to a mature man, to the measure of the stature which belongs to the fullness of Christ.* [14] *As a result, we are no longer to be children, tossed here and there by waves and carried about by every wind of doctrine, by the trickery of men, by craftiness in deceitful scheming;* [15] *but speaking the truth in love, we are to grow up in all aspects into Him who is the head, even Christ, Ephesians 4:13-15*

We find three different age groups identified in 1 John 2. He writes to the little children, to the young men, and to the fathers. This reference has nothing to do with chronological age of the believer, but rather it refers to the level of their spiritual maturity. Children are those who are new to the faith and have yet to grow in the word through the exercising of their senses.

Young men have grown and their zeal for all things related to the Lord sometimes gets them in hot water…not having the seasoning of time and experience. Most have issues to overcome, as they move toward maturity. This is why the wisdom of the fathers is so critical to the body. The fathers impart and mentor those who are less mature.

Mature believers are capable of healthy interpersonal relationships with one another. When we are children, we do childish things; but when we grow up, we establish healthy loving relationships with one another and with God. Mature believers learn how to exercise their gifts to meet the needs of fellow believers in love. Love is the key.

Spiritual Growth Hormone

Growth hormones enable physical bodies to grow and develop into full maturity and adulthood. Without this necessary hormone, growth is stunted and full potential unachieved. When you add strength training, exercise, and a healthy diet, the adult athlete is empowered to effectively out-perform less mature youths in tests of endurance and strength.

A healthy and mature physical body has muscles that work together like a well-oiled machine, unlike the awkwardness of infants or small children. Many athletes have successfully improved the performance of their bodies with the help of a personal trainer.

The adage goes, practice makes perfect. With the guidance of those who are more knowledgeable, we can improve the performance of our body. However, one small injury can diminish the capability and strength of the injured athlete. A pulled muscle, tear, or dislocated joint can cripple and impede the effective movement of the body.

Fivefold Ministry: The Body Builders

If a personal trainer can prepare the body of an athlete to perform effectively, who then can assist the body of believers in their struggle to be perfected? Where are the personal trainers of the church?

"So, Christ himself gave the apostles, the prophets, the evangelists, the pastors and teachers, to equip His people for works of service, so that the body of Christ may be built up until we all reach unity in the faith and in the knowledge of the Son of God and become mature, attaining to the whole measure of the fullness of Christ." Ephesians 4:11-13

Church is not just a social entity; it is a living, breathing organism. This organism is a body, it is the body of Christ. We are each individual members of His body. There are many members, but there is just one body.

Unity is the spiritual growth hormone that strengthens and empowers the members of the body to grow up into Him; into the fullness of who He created us to live and move and have our being.

Behold, how good and how pleasant it is For brothers to dwell together in unity! ² It is like the precious oil upon the head, Coming down upon the beard, Even Aaron's beard, Coming down upon the edge of his robes. ³ It is like the dew of Hermon Coming down upon the mountains of Zion; For there the Lord commanded the blessing—life forever. Psalms 133:1-3

Unity (the spiritual growth hormone) empowers and facilitates church growth. It promotes the overall maturity of the corporate body. The members and the body, as a whole, are thereby empowered to achieve their full potential in Christ. Without unity, the church remains weak and ineffective.

God's blessing comes as we learn to dwell together. When we learn how to encourage, support, and love one another it is mutually and corporately beneficial to all. Healthy interpersonal relationships develop as we grow in grace, authority, and maturation.

Where are the body builders of the church? It is the personal responsibility of fivefold ministers to build up the body, perfect the saints, and guide them from infancy to maturity. It is in maturity and unity that we have the hope of attaining perfection, fulfilling our call.

From the parishioner to the pastor,

From the infant to the spiritually mature,

From the home group to the mega church....

Each individual member of the body is important,

Harmony and unity of the body of Christ are crucial.

Why is unity so important? Being of one mind and one spirit makes us a powerful force to be reckoned with; but disharmony cripples the flow of the church's spiritual power.

Each member is significant to the healthy functioning of the church. What does a healthy church body look like and how do we subscribe to better health? Let us revisit the scripture in John 17:22-23.

"The glory which You have given Me I have given to them, that they may be one, just as We are one; [23] *I in them and You in Me, that they may be perfected in unity, so that the world may know that You sent Me, and loved them, even as You have loved Me." John 17:22-23*

So that we may be "perfected" in unity. While one may argue that there is none perfect but Jesus Christ, we find that the word "perfected" from this text in the original Greek means to be made complete or finished. Perfection, or the completion of the body is accomplished through unity.

What differentiates a healthy church body from an unhealthy one? Some may remember a song made popular years ago by a Christian singing group, Jars of Clay. The song, "They Will Know We Are Christians By Our Love," was originally written by a Catholic priest, Peter Scholtes in 1968. Of course, the song is based upon the scripture found in John 13:34-35:

"A new commandment I give to you, that you love one another, even as I have loved you, that you also love one another. "By this all men will know that you are My disciples, if you have love for one another."

Our relationships and attitudes play key roles in the health and effective functioning of the body of Christ; so also do maturation and the proper positioning of its members.

Have you ever had a joint out of place? It hurts! The body of Christ hurts too when one of its members is out of place or tries to function in a role they were not created to perform. That is why it is crucial that pastors and other fivefold ministry leaders understand the basic anatomy and physiology of a healthy church.

As a child, I had firsthand experience watching the construction of my family home. My mother and father built three different homes, but I was too young to remember much about the first two. However, the third home I do remember.

Once the foundation was poured and the basement blocks were laid, they began adding the floor and then framed up the walls. I remember watching them carefully measure and measure again before beginning to cut the two by four studs. For it to fit properly it had to be a precise measurement, and one could not substitute one stud for another.

I also learned about mitering corners, and how careful the carpenter had to be to be sure everything fit properly, the angle had to be just right.

We see Paul uses the analogies of constructing a building, as well as the anatomy of a physical body to explain how the members of the church are related to one another. (See Ephesians 2, 1 Corinthians 12)

Since Paul has opened the door to this analogy, let us examine the concept of the spiritual anatomy of the church.

Intro to Spiritual Anatomy and Physiology

What do anatomy and physiology have to do with the church body? Spiritual anatomy refers to the proper placement of the church members within the framework of the local body. We would not place the choir director in the maintenance dept. unless they had the gifts and talents to fulfill both positions.

Likewise, we would probably not place the tone-deaf Sunday School teacher in the choir. The gifts, talents, calling, and purpose of the individual church members will determine the roles they can effectively play within the local church.

Physiology refers to the individual characteristics that enable members to work effectively together, or not work together. While we may all be a part of the same local church body, some members relate more closely to one another than others. People who have like interests or are similar in age will be more likely to develop closer relationships than those who do not. Often bible study groups form around people who have similar interests, marital status, or age. Nevertheless, we are all important and significant to the body of believers.

Your heart cannot do the work of your lungs, nor your lungs the work of your heart. Both the heart and the lungs are equally important and must cooperate with one another to provide for the body's need for oxygen. So, it is with the body of Christ, we need each other.

It is the role of fivefold ministry leaders to mentor, educate, and position the members of the body in proper alignment with God's intentions. It is their job to teach the appropriate relationship skills that make unity possible, concepts that yield fruit, the fruit of the spirit.

But the fruit of the Spirit is love, joy, peace, patience, kindness, goodness, faithfulness, gentleness, self-control; against such things there is no law. Galatians 5:22-23

The fruit of the spirit is evidence of growing in spiritual maturity. Babies do not give birth to babies, reproduction or the bearing of fruit requires maturity. When we plant seedlings in the garden, we do not expect an immediate harvest. In some cases, bearing fruit takes years. Take for instance, the apple tree. It requires patience, water, and nutrients. It does not grow to maturity and begin producing apples overnight. It is a process that takes time.

Likewise, growing up in the Lord is a process that requires patience and proper nutrition. The individual believer with the help of the fivefold ministry gifts must take responsibility for personal spiritual growth. We will discuss the role of fivefold ministries in greater detail later in this book.

How do we move from hate to love, from sadness to joy, and from controversy to peace? We begin by cultivating fruit through a healthy, intimate relationship with our Father.

Chapter Two:

Becoming One

Who we hang out with, who we associate with or spend time with is important. We can influence others; likewise, we can be influenced by the company we keep. We can conform to the world or be transformed.

> *And do not be conformed to this world, but be transformed by the renewing of your mind, so that you may prove what the will of God is, that which is good and acceptable and perfect. Romans 12:2*

I have heard that spouses frequently resemble one another after years of living together. Others have commented that they can match dogs with their owners after comparing their physical characteristics. Whether you agree or not, there is some biblical truth to the fact that we begin resembling those we associate with.

> Proverbs 13:20a tells us, *"He who walks with wise men will be wise..."*

The wise hang out with God and develop an intimate relationship with Him. Healthy relationships with others produce spiritual fruit as the legitimate byproducts of a mature relationship with the Father. Likewise, friends of questionable reputation can have a negative effect on our character.

> *The righteous is a guide to his neighbor, But the way of the wicked leads them astray. Proverbs 12:26*

> *Do not be deceived: "Bad company corrupts good morals." 1 Corinthians 15:33*

Where did the concept of unity have its origin? Was it in Ephesians 4:3 where Paul wrote:

being diligent to preserve the unity of the Spirit in the bond of peace.

The word "unity" in this reference is the Greek word, henotes. It means, "oneness" (unity), especially *"God-produced unity (oneness)* between believers i.e. the harmony from sharing *likeness of nature with the Lord."[1]*

Paul is talking about coming together in harmony, a harmony that is produced from sharing the same spiritual DNA, the likeness of God. Later in this same chapter he writes:

until we all attain to the unity of the faith, and of the knowledge of the Son of God, to a mature man, to the measure of the stature which belongs to the fullness of Christ. Ephesians 4:13

Here he speaks of coming together as one in a like-minded faith. This is not a reference to church doctrine, denomination, or a result of church regulations. The word faith here is, by definition, being persuaded by God of His guarantee. Coming together in unity, one-minded, through the divine revelation of our God and Father. We become like minded through a deeper revelation of the mind of God.

"Let this attitude be in you which was also in Christ Jesus" Philippians 2:5

The King James version actually says, let this "mind" be in you. We are encouraged to be like-minded by allowing God, or even seeking God, for a revelation of himself. When we each come to maturity in the knowledge of Him, His thoughts and His nature, we also become like-minded. We then become like-minded with not only God, but with one another.

---

[1] Strong's Greek: 1775

While this is a notable reference to the topic of unity, it is not where it is first mentioned. Did the concept originate in the upper room where it is referenced that they came together in one accord? In Acts 2 we see that the disciples were all together in one place. They were all waiting for the promise as Jesus had instructed them before His ascent to the throne.

Actually, this is not the first reference to the concept of becoming one. To fully understand unity, we must begin in the beginning, as "in the beginning" where God spoke, and it was as He said. The first reference to unity can be found in Genesis.

The first verse that popped into your mind may have been Genesis 2:24b, "… they shall become one flesh." However, another verse that is meaningful here is found later in Genesis 11.

> *The Lord said, "Behold, they are one people, and they all have the same language. And this is what they began to do, and now nothing which they purpose to do will be impossible for them." Genesis 11:6*

While they may have become one, their heart was not right with God and their intentions were not in alignment with God either. Unity is power, for good or for evil.

Defining Unity

If you search the original Greek dictionary for the word unity, you may see definitions such as "oneness", or "in harmony". The Merriam Webster dictionary reveals something similar. However, I like the definition that Pastor Robert Roberts of Grand Blanc, Michigan shared with me recently,

> "Unity: A supernatural work of the Holy Spirit that unites the body of Christ in harmony of function and purpose in order that the will of God can be performed."

I like that, unity….so that the will of God can be performed. I also learned what unity is not; it is not the same as uniformity.

Uniformity attempts to make all things alike, as in a cookie cutter replica. Unity embraces divinely designed diversity.

We are each created uniquely different, yet we become unified as one in Christ. That does not mean we all must look alike, act alike, or sound alike. Rather, we respect and celebrate each individual's gifts, talents, and personality. We bring the gift of our own uniqueness to the table to share with our brothers and sisters in Christ.

You may be wondering in the midst of all this diversity, how we may become one. I assure you it is not through uniformity as in, all ushers must wear black. That may create a similar appearance on the surface, but it speaks nothing of the individual inside.

It is not accomplished through doctrines, rules, and regulations either. That type of mandate may address certain social behaviors, causing us to act the same; but again, it does not truly make us one in mind. It actually lends itself to the potential of manipulation, control, and abuse.

This concept of oneness is difficult to grasp. If we remember that God the Father, God the Son, and God the Holy Spirit are all one in the form of the Trinity, we can begin to grasp the concept of oneness.

Years ago, when I was teaching children the concept of trinity, I would use an egg to illustrate the concept of three in one. The shell is the shell and will always be the shell. The white is the white, and the yolk is equally unique, and it has different characteristics from the other two. However, the three in one become just one egg.

More recently, I was teaching a six-week class at my church for adults. As we got to know one another, it became apparent that we had a BBQ connoisseur in our midst. Toward the end of the study, he offered to make some of his special BBQ chicken for the class.

Now the chicken alone was a delight to be sure, but the meal would not have been complete without the salad, bread, potatoes, deviled eggs, and dessert. We each chose one dish to add to the menu, and together our individual contributions completed the delicious meal.

Likewise, we must each contribute our own individual uniqueness to the whole to make the church complete. Every member has a gift, and is a gift, to the body. Every member is important and vital.

How do we become unified without sacrificing individuality? To make matters worse, the church is struggling with some of the same questions. How, in a society that is becoming increasingly more secular, can the church remain relevant and remain the church? Must we conform to today's culture? If so, at what point do we stop being relevant as the church and start becoming just another social organization? Keep reading; answers will follow.

We Are Better Together

We may live in different parts of the globe. We may speak a different language. We may have different skin colors and different cultural roots; yet we are all one. We are all members of the same family of God.

Each of us is an integral part of His body. From the youngest to the oldest, from the richest to the poorest, from those who are illiterate to those who have attained degrees in higher education, we are all one. We are each connected to God, and to one another, through relationships.

> *For if either of them falls, the one will lift up his companion. But woe to the one who falls when there is not another to lift him up.[11] Furthermore, if two lie down together they keep warm, but how can one be warm alone?[12] And if one can overpower him who is alone, two can resist him. A cord of three strands is not quickly torn apart. Ecclesiastes 4:10-12*

In the US, sports are very important to the American people. Some enjoy golf, while others prefer football, baseball, soccer, or basketball. Golfers have one great disadvantage. If they are having a bad day, they play poorly and there is no remedy. Their score will reflect whatever they do or do not do.

However, those who play one of the other team sports have a decided advantage in that if they are having a bad day, a team member can come along and help out. They support one another, and where one lacks, another may excel. They work together. Just because one person messes up, it does not mean the whole game is lost, for others can help fill in the gap.

Not forsaking the assembling of ourselves together, as the manner of some is; but exhorting one another: and so much the more, as ye see the day approaching. Hebrews 10:25

Some feel they can "do church" from their home, without the benefit of a church body. Perhaps they attend internet church from the comfort of their living room or watch evangelists on their computer. There is nothing wrong with streaming services, especially in the case of one who is ill and unable to attend because of family or work obligations. However, know that at best it may sustain you, but it will not help you grow. We need one another, we need fellowship, we need a support system, and we need someone to whom we can be accountable.

I have been trying to get myself into a workout routine. However, things come up and I forget to do what I have committed myself to do. It is easy to allow other circumstances to crowd out our day and rob us of our time to complete what we set out to do.

The same thing can happen in planning our time of devotions and prayer. We can start out on the right foot, but sometimes we find that things come up and we slowly drift away, allowing life to crowd out our time with the Lord.

This is precisely why it is important to be a part of a team, a church, or a family. It is important to be accountable to someone.

For instance, when trying to get back into shape it is helpful to join an exercise group, or even hire a personal coach. They hold us accountable, and they keep reminding us to follow through with our routine.

You may think of them as your own personal cheering squad, urging you to go further and do better. Even in our study of the word, it is helpful to make ourselves accountable to others in achieving our goals for bible study and prayer.

This is why God put us together in families and appointed a shepherd to care for the sheep. Together we can be more, do more, and accomplish more. There is power in aligning ourselves with likeminded people.

The body of Christ consists of all believers who have accepted Jesus as their personal savior, regardless of skin color, where we live or what language we speak. Collectively, we are each individual members of the body of Christ and we have each been adopted into the family of God as His children. We are one body, in Christ; and one family in God.

Paul spoke further of us becoming one:

> *[29] for no one ever hated his own flesh, but nourishes and cherishes it, just as Christ also does the church, [30] because we are members of His body. [31] For this reason a man shall leave his father and mother and shall be joined to his wife, and the two shall become one flesh [32] This mystery is great; but I am speaking with reference to Christ and the church. Ephesians 5:29-32*

We are to nourish and cherish our flesh. This flesh is not only our own flesh, but also the flesh of our brothers and sisters in the Lord. We become one flesh, one body, one spirit, and one mind. We are to use the love of God and the gifts He has given, to provide for one another. We see this enacted in the early church of Acts.

And the congregation of those who believed were of one heart and soul; and not one of them claimed that anything belonging to him was his own, but all things were common property to them. Acts 4:32

I am not telling you that you need to sell all of your belongings and give them to the church, but I am saying that we are to have the same care for one another as we have for ourselves. The bottom line is this; we are to love one another.

We will continue to discuss how we are to minister to one another in love in the remainder of this book.

Chapter Three:

Blueprint of the Future, Vision

In a previous chapter I shared of how my father and mother built three separate family homes. I remember the discussion that began the building process of house number three. It started with the development of a vision.

Actually, it began with, "how could you sell our house," but I digress. Mom and Dad quickly came into agreement, as they always do. So, they began the process of building a new and bigger home for our family.

They discussed what they each desired in our new home, then they committed the plan to paper. The blueprint used to build the home was their vision. It made the plan plain and clear enabling others, skilled tradesmen, to participate in its fulfillment.

> *Then the LORD answered me and said, "Record the vision and inscribe it on tablets, That the one who reads it may run."*
> *Habakkuk 2:2*

While the completion of our home required the assistance of a brick layer, a carpenter, and many others, it first began with a vision.

Prophetic Revelation

What is prophetic revelation? It is the ability to foresee the future. It is the visualization of something that has not yet taken place. It is part of God's unmanifested plan revealed to man in advance of its fulfillment. What is the purpose of this prophetic revelation?

A prophetic revelation or vision is given by God and it enables those who hear it time to prepare. It is foreknowledge of a coming event. It may come as a warning, or it may come so that those who hear it may participate in the fulfillment. It is the impartation of divine wisdom and knowledge.

> *Where there is no revelation, people cast off restraint; but blessed is the one who heeds wisdom's instruction. Proverbs 29:18 NIV*

I think of Joseph, preparing a nation for a coming famine. It was the foreknowledge of what was to come that gave him the wisdom to orchestrate the remedy. It was Joseph's gift of prophetic insight and divine wisdom exercised on Egypt's behalf that saved his own family from certain starvation!

The Power to Manifest Vision

Vision teamed with faith and action is powerful. Many years ago, I refrain from saying how many, I read a true story about Walt Disney and the creation of Space Mountain. It seems that Disneyland had just opened and had only one ride.

A gardener tending the grounds observed Walt sitting and starring at the undeveloped land in front of him. Finally, the gardener became concerned. He asked Walt, "How are you?" Without looking up, Walt responded, "Fine." So, the gardener persisted, "What are you doing?" Walt responded, "Looking at my mountain. I see it right there."

He shared his vision of "the mountain" with architects who drew up the architectural plans and began the construction. Walt died before the construction of Space Mountain could be completed. Fortunately, we know he had already seen the mountain before the construction had even begun; it was the rest of the world that had to wait until it was completed before we could see it. That is the power of vision. It prophesies of the future.

The Power of Vision

Adding Faith + Action to Vision = Manifested Vision

Faith and action added to vision have the power to make the vision manifest in due season. We are talking about coming into agreement with a God-given vision; and adding faith and action to what God has given. The power of vision is well illustrated in the biblical story of Jacob and the spotted lambs in Ge.30:25-43.

Laban and Jacob discussed the wages to be given to Jacob for his labor. Jacob requested all the speckled and spotted among the sheep, and every black lamb. In addition, he requested the speckled and spotted among the goats and Laban agreed to his proposal.

Jacob then peeled white stripes in rods from the poplar and almond trees and laid them in the water trough where the flocks came to drink and mate. They would see the stripes and then they reproduced striped, spotted, and all black offspring.

If the weaker livestock came to reproduce, he would remove the rods. If the stronger and healthy ones came to drink and reproduce, he laid the rods in the trough. Therefore, his flocks grew in number and strength. They produced what they saw. That is the power of vision in action.

Vision, prophetic revelation, and the needed gift of divine wisdom are gifts from God to His people. How can we, as Paul said, run our race and set our eyes on the goal if we cannot visualize the goal? The goal is spiritually discerned and visualized by the eyes of our heart.

> *I pray that the eyes of your heart may be enlightened, so that you will know what is the hope of His calling what are the riches of the glory of His inheritance in the saints, Ephesians 1:18*

God wants you to see the vision prophetically, to know it in your heart, so that you can run to see it fulfilled. The vision is spiritually discerned and walked out by faith. If you could see it in the natural it would not be faith. Paul encouraged us to run the race that is set before us.

> *Therefore, since we have so great a cloud of witnesses surrounding us, let us also lay aside every encumbrance and the sin which so easily entangles us, and let us run with endurance the race that is set before us, Hebrews 12:1*

Courage Required

Living by faith and running the race is not for cowards. Stepping out of your comfort zone to pursue the dream requires courage. If it were easy, it wouldn't be God. God's dream for you is big and He wants to partner with you as you walk by faith to achieve the dream.

I remember a season in my life that was quite difficult; we have all had those seasons. We have been there, done that, and have the battle scars to prove it. This was one of the seasons when the events in my life, had they been recorded in song lyrics, could have become a hit country song.

Do you know what I mean? I lost my house, my car, my job, my forty-year marriage and most of my possessions. Life events forced me to walk away from my position as a staff pastor in a local church and listen to what the Lord told me to do… rest. Pick up and move with what little I could fit in the back of a van and move to North Carolina. It wasn't even my van; it was my daughter's.

I left the only place I had ever lived. Do you know how hard it is to start over miles from home when you have never lived more than forty miles from your birthplace? I was fifty-eight years old, with little to call my own, uprooted from everything except my daughter and her family who lived in North Carolina.

God said rest and recover, but don't get rooted. I wanted to be rooted, I wanted a place to call my own. That was not the prescription for the season. I learned to let go and trust God. I rested and began to recover... as I had little other choice but to trust and obey as the old song lyrics go. God wanted to teach me that He could provide all that I would need.

Living for God is not for cowards, it takes courage to walk out God's plan. If you don't have courage, God will teach you. That is what He did for me. I really wanted to rely on a job to provide for me, but He taught me that He had more than enough to provide for every need. I do not regret what I walked through; in fact, I am grateful. It has made me who I am today.

It is through grace, by faith that you are called to come out of the world and into the light of His love, to fulfill your kingdom purpose. I do not recommend leaving everything and starting over, but if God calls you to it, as you have probably heard, He will bring you through it. God wants to be your source.

I remember one day, during that one-year sabbatical that God had me on in North Carolina, I was having a pity party and was whining to God. I am sure you have never done that, but I must confess I did and on more than one occasion. I complained that I had nothing of my own; and did not see a future for myself....my life was just on hold.

That is when I started hearing these questions in my spirit:

- Do you have a bed to sleep in and a warm place to live?

- Do you have food to eat and a family to love?

- Do you truly lack any good thing?

That is when I had to confess, I had all that I truly needed. Then I heard, "there are many sleeping in the streets that wish they had what you do." It was humbling, and I was ashamed. I truly did not lack, and God had been very good to me. I repented.

Then I heard these final thoughts, "I have treasures on the path where you are, that are just for today. If you do not gather them, they will be lost forever." I knew those treasures were the memories I was making with my kids and grandkids. I will always be grateful for the time God gave me to make memories while my grandchildren were still young.

I learned much during that one-year sabbatical, but most of all I learned I could trust God. I thought I had faith before, but my level of trust had grown exponentially. Little did I know this was only the beginning of my faith walk into the unknown with God.

The Called-Out Ones

A biblical hero who had the courage to walk out the dream by faith was Abraham.

> Now the LORD said to Abram,
> "Go forth from your country,
> And from your relatives
> And from your father's house,
> To the land which I will show you;
>
> And I will make you a great nation,
> And I will bless you,
> And make your name great;
> And so you shall be a blessing;
>
> And I will bless those who bless you,
> And the one who curses you I will curse.
> And in you all the families of the earth will be blessed."
> Genesis 12:1-3

God called Abram out to fulfill the purpose for which he was created. It required sacrifice and trust, it required courage and commitment. It required his walking away from the many he knew and did life with, to pursue his destiny.

Know that answering the call of God to pursue the dream will not always be met with optimism by others. When you disrupt your routine to change your course, it may affect how you interact with the others with whom you are doing life.

They may not be happy or supportive. Your change of course may force them to reassess themselves and make necessary adjustments. Change is hard for many and they may resist. Nevertheless, you must stay focused on what God is calling you to do and allow God to be God.

Jesus was the son of a carpenter, He had brothers, sisters, and a mother that everyone in the neighborhood knew. The people He grew up with found the transition He made into ministry troubling at best. Everyone that is, except perhaps Mary. She had a prophetic revelation of who He would become. She had been forewarned.

As He walked about teaching and working miracles, those who had known Him as a child were skeptical to say the least. Because of their skepticism and unacceptance, He was unable to work as freely in His own hometown. He addresses this in Luke 4:24.

Change is hard and not everyone is happy about change when it comes. If the people you do life with truly want what is best for you, they will hang in and transition with you. For example, parents spend at least eighteen years raising their children. As a young adult, the grown child will get a job, go to school, and pursue a life of their own. The parents must transition in their relationship with their child.

Some will celebrate what God is doing in your life, and others not so much. While a few remain at our side for a lifetime, others for only a season. It is important to know the difference. When we agree to accept God's call, we must be prepared that there may be some collateral damage. We cannot control how others will respond.

Abram and his family had to leave their family, friends, and neighbors to pursue the dream. There is a price to pay, but Abram trusted the Lord. He knew he had a prophetic future to fulfill. God would make of him a nation and a blessing. God had called Abram to come out from among them.

The Greek word for church is Ekklesia. It means the called-out ones and they gather together to govern in a locality. Jesus called His disciples to come out from among the crowd to follow Him. Members of the modern-day church have been called to come out from the world of darkness and into His light, forming the body of Christ. No longer of the world, we are now members of a new kingdom, the kingdom of God.

God called us out to lead us into the land He has promised. It is His Kingdom, spiritually discerned and faithfully pursued, by all who hear the call. So, what next? Where do we go and what do we do to fulfill our purpose in Him? It begins with the spiritually discerned vision.

> *Enlarge the place of your tent; Stretch out the curtains of your dwellings, spare not; Lengthen your cords And strengthen your pegs. [3] "For you will spread abroad to the right and to the left. And your descendants will possess nations And will resettle the desolate cities. [4] "Fear not, for you will not be put to shame; And do not feel humiliated, for you will not be disgraced; But you will forget the shame of your youth, And the reproach of your widowhood you will remember no more. [5] "For your husband is your Maker, Whose name is the Lord of hosts; And your Redeemer is the Holy One of Israel, Who is called the God of all the earth. Isaiah 54:2-5*

What can we as the called-out ones of the modern-day church take away from this scripture? Enlarge your vision to include what God intends to do in you and through you. Don't limit God by your lack of faith and action. Do not be afraid, God is working in you and through you to bring it to pass. The three main points of this scripture are:

- Enlarge your tent

- Expand your borders

- Set the course

Let us discuss these concepts in greater detail.

It Begins with A God-Given Vision

Enlarging your tent and expanding your borders will involve thinking outside the box. If your dream or vision is something you can achieve on your own, chances are it is not God's full purpose for you. God's plans are so big it requires His divine intervention to accomplish.

> *For I know the plans that I have for you,' declares the Lord, 'plans for welfare and not for calamity to give you a future and a hope. Then you will call upon Me and come and pray to Me, and I will listen to you. You will seek Me and find Me when you search for Me with all your heart. Jeremiah 29:11-13*

Give God permission to reveal His perfect purpose for you without the hindrance of self-limiting beliefs. Trust God. Do not allow fear or the expectations of others to limit the vision you receive from God. You will want to see clearly through your eyes of faith; what it is that God wants to do, both in you and through you.

Corporate Vision

Leaders must also seek God's plan and purpose for those they shepherd. Often God's purpose is location sensitive, as in the case of Abraham. He had to go to the place he was called. Also, we see this in the case of Moses and Joseph. Location is critical, one must go where God is calling.

The provision to fulfill the vision is in the location you are called to serve. When it was time for Elijah to move from the riverbed to the widow's house, his provision at the riverbed dried up. He had to go to the location God was calling him to, and provision was awaiting him there.

God is into the Details.

Then you shall erect the tabernacle according to its plan which you have been shown in the mountain. Exodus 26:30

In Exodus 26 we find the explicit instructions given to Moses on the mountain for the creation of the tabernacle. God said, erect it according to its plan. Every minute detail is addressed and to be strictly followed in the construction, much like an architect's blueprint. The plan is birthed in one's mind, then it is recorded and preserved. In biblical days, instructions such as the ten commandments, were etched in stone. Today we are more likely to record the vision in some digital fashion.

Moses was given instructions to build the first tabernacle in the wilderness.

Then the Lord spoke to Moses, saying, [2] "Tell the sons of Israel to raise a contribution for Me; from every man whose heart moves him you shall raise My contribution. [3] This is the contribution which you are to raise from them: gold, silver and bronze, [4] blue, purple and scarlet material, fine linen, goat hair, [5] rams' skins dyed red, porpoise skins, acacia wood, [6] oil for lighting, spices for the anointing oil and for the fragrant incense, [7] onyx stones and setting stones for the ephod and for the breast piece. [8] Let them construct a sanctuary for Me, that I may dwell among them. [9] According to all that I am going to show you, as the pattern of the tabernacle and the pattern of all its furniture, just so you shall construct it. Exodus 25:1-9

The instructions were detailed and precise. King David also received instructions for a temple. He was not allowed to proceed with the construction, but he prepared for it (See 1 Chronicles 22).

Solomon later oversaw the completion of the temple according to the plan given to his father David (See 1 Kings 8). The vision was multigenerational and required preservation and impartation so that others could run to fulfill it. The vision God gives is often so big it requires the cooperation of others to complete.

Casting the Vision

Gaining the cooperation of others in the fulfillment of a vision requires effective communication. In the case of Habakkuk, God obviously felt the written word would most accurately convey His intent. Visionaries of the 21st century have many different media choices by which they may record the vision. Nevertheless, their ability to communicate the vision and engage the assistance of others is crucial.

What does it mean to cast a vision? A vision is a mental image which is imparted (cast) to others through words, pictures, or sound. Effective vision casting is dependent upon good com-munication skills.

Mature leaders must learn how to impart the God given vision so that others will enthusiastically embrace it and willingly participate in its fulfillment. This is much like a coach or a squadron leader who knows how to rally the troops. When members have embraced part ownership of the dream and have willingly accepted responsibility for its fulfillment, the impartation is then complete.

Healthy and mature leaders can communicate the vision effectively; engaging others without the use of manipulation or control. Mature visionaries step out in faith trusting the Holy Spirit to draw those of His choosing to participate.

If the Holy Spirit does not draw them, you do not want to engage them by other means; that would be a recipe for disaster. Note this, timing is crucial. Visions have an appointed time and if others are not willing to participate, it may simply not be their right time.

When you engage others in the fulfillment of a vision, it is important to frequently reinforce the intended goal. Make certain the bullseye of the target remains crystal clear for all to see. Most of us have played telephone as children. The message whispered to the first hearer is often vastly different from the message the final person receives. This increases the likeliness of mis-communication and the potential for error.

The longer it takes to complete the vision, the greater chance there is for error. Maintaining clear lines of communication and reinforcing the goal from time to time are crucial to keeping everyone on the same page.

Habakkuk was told to write it down. He was told to make it plain so that the one who reads it can run with it. Documentation of the plan will clarify the vision and keep everyone together on task.

We have discussed personal vision as well as corporate vision in this chapter. Both are important. Our personal vision will help us identify where we fit in to the corporate vision.

It is important that we discover who we are in Christ, what our purpose is, and how we fit into the intricate plan of God on earth. We each have a part to play, and it is crucial to the overall plan for the church and for one another. We need each other.

Chapter Four:

Spiritual Anatomy

Finding where you fit into God's overall plan is crucial. Remember the scripture in Jeremiah 29:11? God knows the plans He has for you, … plans to give you a future. That is because He created you for a specific purpose. God is not only purposeful, but intentional; He does not make mistakes.

Do you know His plan and purpose for you? Understanding how the body of Christ fits together helps us better identify our own personal role within the church. Where do you fit into God's overall plan for the kingdom? Let's examine God's blueprint for the church. I like to call it spiritual anatomy.

An architect can identify flaws in the construction of a building because he or she has the original blueprint. The accepted standard is drawn up in a physical diagram that the architect can visualize. The physical building is, or at least should be, a mirror image of the original blueprint. Anything in the physical reproduction that does not appear in the blueprint is potentially a flaw or error.

A few years ago, long before I began working at Vision International University, I supported myself and my family by working as a registered nurse. When I was in nursing school, one of my favorite subjects was anatomy and physiology.

Physical Anatomy

A comprehensive understanding of the makeup of the healthy human body is fundamental to helping the sick recover. One must first understand and visualize how it functions normally, before it is possible to identify potential flaws or abnormalities.

I studied the anatomy and physiology of the human body. I learned about the various bones, organs and body systems that form it. Understanding how each organ interacts with others was crucial. Properly assessing my patients was dependent upon my ability to identify anything that was abnormal.

During my nursing school studies, I became fascinated by the intricacy with which the human body was created. Each system had its own specific components; they worked closely together with other systems. The systems all needed each other to fulfill the role for which they were created. Cooperation of the various systems with one another was essential to the health and wellbeing of the individual.

The circulatory system relies on the respiratory system, and the nervous system depends on the skeletal system and so forth. No one body system is capable of functioning independently of the others. They need each other even as we need each other.

Connections

Even as the human body is made up of many different members, so is the body of Christ. As the body of Christ, it is important that we understand how and where our members fit together. We need to understand each person's role and his or her responsibilities. How does that role and function fit seamlessly with the others to support the individual members of the body?

> *But now God has placed the members, each one of them, in the body, just as He desired.* [19] *If they were all one member, where would the body be?* [20] *But now there are many members, but one body.* [21] *And the eye cannot say to the hand, "I have no need of you"; or again the head to the feet, "I have no need of you."* [22] *On the contrary, it is much truer that the members of the body which seem to be weaker are necessary;*
>
> [23] *and those members of the body which we deem less honorable, on these we bestow more abundant honor, and our less presentable members become much more presentable,* [24] *whereas our more presentable members have no need of it.*

But God has so composed the body, giving more abundant honor to that member which lacked,

[25] so that there may be no division in the body, but that the members may have the same care for one another. 1 Corinthians 12:18-25.

How does my calling, purpose, and gifts benefit my brothers and sisters in the Lord? How do I relate and function in relationship to other church members to create a strong, healthy, and growing body? Understanding God's blueprint for a healthy and mature church body is crucial if we are to become one in spirit, soul, and body.

Just as there is a blueprint for the construction of a physical building, there is also a blueprint for a physical body. We call it anatomy.

The Body's Blueprint

To begin our discussion of this important topic, I would like to refer to the scripture in Ezekiel 37 regarding the dry bones. We see in this text that God had a conversation with Ezekiel about the dry, dead bones lying about in the valley. He told Ezekiel to prophesy to the bones.

It is important to note that the concept of prophesying to the bones did not originate with Ezekiel, but with God. God told him what to say and what to prophesy, Ezekiel did not think this up on his own, but he spoke what he heard his Father speak. We must come into agreement with the words and the will of the Father. John in chapter 12:49-50 relates these words of Jesus:

For I did not speak on My own initiative, but the Father Himself who sent Me has given Me a commandment as to what to say and what to speak. [50] I know that His commandment is eternal life; therefore the things I speak, I speak just as the Father has told Me."

Again, in John 5:19:

Therefore Jesus answered and was saying to them, "Truly, truly, I say to you, the Son can do nothing of Himself, unless it is something He sees the Father doing; for whatever the Father does, these things the Son also does in like manner.

Therefore, Ezekiel prophesied to the dead bones and they came together. The illustration of dead bones coming together is in reference to the promise of God in the preceding chapter. He promised the restoration of the nation of Israel; they would be gathered together again from the places where they had been scattered.

Secondly, we can see this representation being carried even further to symbolize the restoration of the body of Christ. The members of His body were once dead in their sin, but they are promised resurrection and newness of life in Christ Jesus. (See the commentary of Matthew Henry on Ezekiel 37.)

Therefore, we can reason that the bones are representatives of the members of the body, as are you and I. We are the bones of the body of Christ.

Joints

As the bones of the body, we come together at junctions better known in the body as joints. Bone comes together with bone, and they meet in a relationship to one another. Therefore, the joints are the relationships we have with one another in the body of Christ.

The needs of the body are met within those relationships. Think of the relationships that develop within the scope of a small group. We have the opportunity to minister and support one another within the relationships we develop there with one another.

From whom the whole body, fitly joined together and compacted by that which every joint supplieth, according to the effectual working in the measure of every part, maketh

increase of the body unto the edifying of itself in love.
Ephesians 4:16

That verse is powerful; it contains enough spiritual food for a whole month of Sundays! Therefore, we might first refer to an interlinear bible to determine the original meaning. For instance, the word "whole" in the original Greek means: to join closely together, to frame together, parts of a building, or the members of a body.

We could say that the "whole body" is the members of the body that have been framed or fit together. The verse repeats this thought in the next phrase, "fitly joined together. Just as a builder constructs a framework for the building by joining the boards together at joints, so must the body of Christ be fit together. The members (bones) must come into proper alignment and location within the body.

If the framework of a building is to fit together properly, one must measure and adjust the boards individually. They will then fit together snuggly to support one another in their proper place.

If the angle is incorrect, the union between the two boards is compromised. Strength comes from the proper placement of each one. If the boards are connected incorrectly, the result can be disastrous. Each one must be prepared and placed into its proper location for maximum stability and functionality of the unit as a whole.

This same analogy works for the physical body. Try fitting a hipbone into a shoulder socket, or the index finger into the hip, it does not work effectively. The bones must fit together in their proper place. The place for which they were created. Bones that are out of place are referred to as disjointed.

When a joint becomes disjointed, it causes the whole body to feel discomfort and pain. The ability of the body to function effectively is compromised by the misplaced bone. Each bone in our body was created to fit in a specific place to fulfill a specific purpose.

Have you ever seen someone try to function in a gift or role in the church that was clearly not theirs? For instance, the church member that is highly gifted as an usher or sound technician may make a very poor administrator. The Sunday school teacher may be an excellent educator but should not attempt to lead the church choir if they cannot carry a tune.

People who are out of place or missing cause the whole body to suffer. Therefore, we should not forsake the assembling of ourselves, for each member is needed. Each one supplies a gift and nourishment for the body. With one part missing, the body as a whole is less effective.

Let us look further into this scripture, *"fitly joined together and compacted by that which every joint supplieth."* Bones or members that are fit together properly, create joints that are not only compacted, but also supply the needs of the body.

How could your upper arm function properly if it were not for the lower arm? They must not only be present, but they must also meet at the proper joint in order for both bones to work together. Pushing, pulling, or picking up another object would not be possible unless both bones are in place and healthy. When both are in place, when both are healthy and functioning properly, the joint supplies the needs of the body and gives it full functionality.

If one member of the body becomes sick or diseased, then it affects that one part; but it also affects the body as a whole. If I should stub my toe or step on a nail, the strain of trying to walk without further pain takes a toll on my whole body. When one member of the body of Christ hurts, we all hurt.

So how do joints supply the needs of others? We minister to fellow members of the body within relationships. We interact by consoling, praying, and supporting others. We utilize our gifts and talents, sharing with one another as we come together in relationships. We are empowered by our spiritual gifts to minister to the needs of others. Therefore, our relationships are very important.

Sinews?

Ezekiel prophesied to the bones, and they came together at joints. The joints without support are vulnerable to dislocation; to strengthen the union of bones God added sinews. Sinews is not a word we typically use in our conversations today.

Physical Anatomy

Bones meet at joints. Joints are strengthened by ligaments and tendons

What are sinews? Strong's concordance defines the word as a "tendon". Tendons and ligaments support the union of two bones at a joint.

So then, how do our relationships with one another receive support?

According to Colossians 2:19:

> *And not holding fast to the head, from whom the entire body, being supplied and held together by the joints and ligaments, grows with a growth which is from God.*

The source of our strength and support is Jesus Christ, who is the head of the body. From him comes the nourishment that supplies all of our needs. As long as we remain in Him, and He in us, we have a continuous supply to meet every need.

> *[5] I am the vine, you are the branches; he who abides in Me and I in him, he bears much fruit, for apart from Me you can do nothing. John 15:5*

Spiritual Anatomy

relationships= joints
right attitudes = ligaments and tendons

Right attitudes strengthen
our relationships.

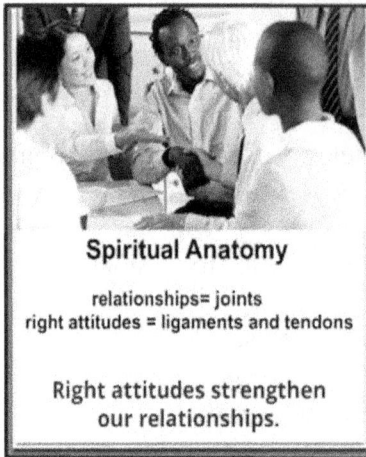

Let us review for a moment. The joints and the ligaments hold the bones of the physical body together. Therefore, in the spiritual body the bones are individual members of the church body that come together in relationships.

What strengthens our relationships with one another? Right attitudes (the ligaments and tendons) when we worship, fellowship, or do life together; it strengthens not only our interpersonal relationships, but the body as a whole. A body of believers with one heart, one mind, and one spirit becomes an empowered body of Christ. We need each other. None of us is whole without the others. We were created for unity and relationship. We must come together in right attitudes toward one another.

For just as we have many members in one body and all the members do not have the same function so we, who are many, are one body in Christ, and individually members one of another. Romans 12:4-5

Flesh and Skin

Once again, in Ezekiel's recount of the body coming together, he tells us of how the bones were covered with flesh and skin. In keeping with the analogy of the human body, what might the flesh and skin represent in the body of Christ?

For one thing, we know that we are held together by a bond of peace. Let us examine yet another scripture that focuses on the concepts presented in this chapter.

With all humility and gentleness, with patience, showing tolerance for one another in love, ³A Spirit in the bond of peace. ⁴There is one body and one Spirit, just as also you were called in one hope of your calling; ⁵one Lord, one faith, one baptism, ⁶one God and Father of all who is over all and through all and in all. Ephesians 4:2-6

We can see here how right attitudes including humility, patience, and love maintained in a bond of peace can strengthen the whole body. The bond of peace might be likened to the covering of flesh.

The ultimate bond however is love. It is the most important unifying factor in the body. We are to love one another, but we also know that the love of God hides a multitude of sins. At the end of the day, love through faith is the primary adhesive holding us all together.

Breath

And he prophesied to the four winds and the breath came into them, and they came alive. The wind symbolized the Spirit of God. Like mouth-to-mouth resuscitation, the breath revived the dead bones and they stood on their feet a mighty army.

In the New Testament, we see the disciples in Acts 2 awaiting the promise of God, and a mighty rushing wind came into the upper room. They were endued with power from on high. The awaited promise had come.

Spiritual Anatomy Conclusion

Some bones are more closely related to one another, have more in common with one another, than others. Some of the bones come together and form a Baptist church; some form a Lutheran church, and some form a Pentecostal or Charismatic church.

Even in one local body, we have many different bones that come together, yet we are not all alike. Not all are noses, ears, or eyes. Not all are the leg, the arm, or the hand. Yet God has placed us together as He wills. What good would a body be if all its members were the same part and function?

> *"If they were all one member, where would the body be? Now there are many members but one body. I Corinthians 12: 19-20*

How do the bones know how to come together in their proper place? We need body builders. God's body builders are the fivefold ministry. They function as the hand of God to equip and strengthen the body.

> *And He gave some as apostles, and some as prophets, and some as evangelists, and some as pastors and teachers, [12] for the equipping of the saints for the work of service, to the building up of the body of Christ; (Ephesians 4:11-12)*

The word "equip" in this verse means to set in place, to fit together, to set in order, to mend, to prepare. Like framing a house or setting a bone. The bones in the body must be fit together in the proper order by God's body building fivefold ministry.

The members of the body must be trained and equipped. Immature believers are not ready to fulfill their callings; they need more mature believers to mentor them, hence the fivefold ministry. Ephesians 4:13 reads that the fivefold ministry needs to train the believers,

> *until we all attain to the unity of the faith, and of the knowledge of the Son of God, to a mature man, to the measure of the stature which belongs to the fullness of Christ. Ephesians 4:13*

From dead bones to lively army, tendons, ligaments, bones, and skin... the body of Christ can be resurrected and walk in the newness of life. Love will hold us all together as one.

Chapter Five:

The Power of a Hand Up

Venturing into unknown territory can be exciting and scary all at the same time. I have to admire the early settlers as they pushed through from the East coast to the West coast with little more than a dream. Those that endured the many difficult challenges and circumstances to overcome, pioneered an opportunity for each of us.

Those that followed built on the foundations that the early pioneers established. You might say they gave each of us a hand up, thus we did not have to trek across the wilderness on our own, to build homes and cities. We were able to build upon the work of others.

Paul spoke in 1 Corinthians 3:5-9:

> *What then is Apollos? And what is Paul? Servants through whom you believed, even as the Lord gave opportunity to each one. ⁶ I planted, Apollos watered, but God was causing the growth. ⁷ So then neither the one who plants nor the one who waters is anything, but God who causes the growth. ⁸ Now he who plants and he who waters are one; but each will receive his own reward according to his own labor. ⁹ For we are God's fellow workers; you are God's field, God's building.*

I think back on my own life and I can see the hand of God sending people into my life to help me through scary and uncharted territory, like my friend Mickie. I had suddenly found myself alone with no confidence or skills to care for myself. I needed help! I needed a hand up. So, God sent me Mickie.

I had never, in almost 60 years, been on my own. Now suddenly, I was. How would I manage? Who would fix the computer, the furnace, the car? I had rarely driven on a busy interstate and <u>never</u>

by myself. My navigation skills were buried in fear of the unknown.

My new friend Mickie learned how to care for herself after the death of her husband; so, she taught me. Mostly, she gave me the confidence that I could manage on my own. She reminded me that I was not really alone, but that God was with me on this adventure.

Remember the children's story about the engine that could? *I think I can, I think I can, I think I can.* Mickie was my cheering squad, standing beside me, guiding me through thick clouds of self-doubt. She kept assuring me that I could do this.

I needed to traverse a lot of unknown territory in the months and years ahead, but I was not alone. So, when a life crisis had me down for the ten count, God sent someone into my life to give me a hand up. She was one of many that God sent to help me along the way.

Jesus knew that as a body of believers, we would be traversing unknown territory. While salvation is instantaneous, perfection is a process. Guides, mentors, and teachers help others progress along this path. We would need help in our journey from worldly ways, customs, and mindsets; to kingdom living. So, He left us with a gift, a hand up if you will, the fivefold ministry. Paul said:

> *and He gave some, apostles, and some prophets, and some evangelists, and some pastors, and teachers. For the Perfecting of the saints, for the work of the ministry, for the edifying of the body of Christ. Ephesians 4:11-12*

As I contemplated how to begin this chapter, I researched what others had already written. I soon discovered there is far less discussion on this topic than say the gifts of the Holy Spirit.

While one may find numerous books on the individual offices within the fivefold ministry, I found little on the fivefold ministry as a whole. Without doubt, there is much to learn and much to gain through an understanding the fivefold ministry. But first a question, "Where did the concept of a five- fold ministry come from?" Let us back up a few verses, starting in verse 4.

There is one body and one Spirit, just as also you were called in one hope of your calling; one Lord, one faith one baptism, one God and Father of all who is over all and through all and in all.

But to each one of us grace was given according to the measure of Christ's gift.

Therefore, it says,

WHEN HE ASCENDED ON HIGH, HE LED CAPTIVE A HOST OF CAPTIVES, AND HE GAVE GIFTS TO MEN."
Ephesians 4:4-8

"To each one of us grace was given", that is not just unmerited favor, that grace is the power of God. We have the power of God operating on the inside of us. Paul also said that Christ gave gifts, and then he goes on to identify the gifts. There are five of them, and they represent a portion of the ministry of the Lord. We also see the ministry gifts mentioned in Corinthians.

"Now there are varieties of gifts, but the same Spirit. [5] And there are varieties of ministries, and the same Lord. [6] There are varieties of effects, but the same God who works all things in all persons." 1 Corinthians 12:4-6

Verse four starts by mentioning varieties of gifts, these are the spiritual gifts that we will discuss in detail in another chapter. The Spiritual gifts are given by Holy Spirit. Do you see that at the end of verse four," *The same spirit*"? Verse five however discusses varieties of ministries, and the same Lord. The Lord Jesus gave ministry gifts as further detailed in Ephesians four.

In 1 Corinthians 12:4, the word, "ministries" in the original Greek, was the word "diakonia". It means, to command, or to execute the commands of others. In modern day lingo one might say they are large and in charge. In other words, the fivefold ministry gifts are the administrative gifts within the body. They are responsible for maintaining order, training, and equipping the body of believers.

This scriptural reference outlines three classifications of gifts as well as identifying the individual member of the godhead that gives the gift. In verse four we have the Holy Spirit giving spiritual gifts. The nine spiritual gifts will be reviewed thoroughly in the next chapter. In verse five, Jesus gives the ministry or administrative gifts.

Finally, in verse six we have the gifts of the Father, known by many as the personality or motivational gifts. The gifts as outlined by Paul come in three classifications, given by the three different members of the godhead or the Trinity. In my first book I coined the phrase, gifts of the Trinity. You can see here why. (Smith, 2013)

The fivefold ministry then, according to Ephesians 4:12 was given, *"For the Perfecting of the saints, for the work of the ministry, for the edifying of the body of Christ."* Many mistakenly think that the members of the fivefold ministry are called to do the ministry in the body, but actually they are called to train and equip the members of the body to do the ministry.

The purpose of the Fivefold ministry

Paul told us their job was to perfect the saints, for the work of the ministry, for the edifying of the body of Christ. When you do a word study in the original Greek you will discover this:

- Perfecting = 2677 katartismos   properly, exact adjustment which describes how (enables) the individual parts to work together in correct order

- Edifying =3619 ikodomé the act of building, (b) a build-ing, (c) met: spiritual advancement, edification [2]

Fivefold ministers construct, fit in place, build up the body; they set the bones in place. Fivefold ministries lead and guide the saints from spiritual infancy to spiritual maturity. They help them find and fulfill the perfect will of God for their life. How?

Jesus was in the process of building a body of believers to form the church, but He needed "construction workers" or body builders to put all things in order according to the plan, the blueprint.

Responsibilities of Fivefold Ministries

Gifts may not be obvious at first, especially in new believers. As new believers grow, mature, and exercise their faith, the gifts begin to flow. It is the role of those in leadership, especially those in the offices of the fivefold ministry, to help each member of the body discover their gift, develop it, and find their own specific place within the body.

As each individual member finds their place and fulfills it, the whole body can mature and grow as the church. If all ministry was the responsibility of the fivefold ministries... very little could be accomplished. The work of the ministry is the responsibility of each individual member.

In my book, *Effective Pastoral Care Ministry in the Local Church*, (Smith, 2016) I go into great detail of how the growth of the local church is stunted when all ministerial duties for the church are the sole responsibility of the pastor. When the lay ministry steps in to help shoulder the responsibilities under the pastor's supervision, growth is not only possible, but probable.

We can see evidence of bible heroes needing help with the care of the sheep; take Moses. Remember the battle when Moses had to hold up his staff? When he grew tired and tried to lower his arms

---

[2] (See your Strong's concordance for more information.)

for a rest, the troops would begin losing the battle. The strain or the weight of the task was too great for him to bare by himself; therefore, Aaron and Hur supported his arms until the battle was won.

Again, we see another illustration, when Moses' father-in-law came to visit him in the wilderness to deliver his wife and children. He observed Moses judging the people from morning to night. Jethro cautioned that the job was too great for one man to do alone; he needed help.

Moses adhered to the advice of Jethro, choosing godly leaders to act as under shepherds and delegated authority to them to act on his behalf. Jethro presented a good idea, not necessarily a God idea, as many of the chosen leaders later became problematic for Moses (see Numbers 11)

Often the diagram of a hand is used to illustrate these offices. The thumb is the apostle, the forefinger is the prophet. Note these two offices often work very closely together, like Moses and Aaron. Let us examine more closely each individual member of this team.

The Apostle

The Apostle in the Greek is Apostolos meaning one who is sent; much like our modern-day ambassadors. They are commissioned with a message and empowered with supernatural powers.

The apostle establishes new kingdom ministries, preparing the foundation work and raising up local leadership. The apostle then encourages and strengthens those he oversees. He is also called to bring discipline when the need arises.

The apostle may evangelize, pastor, prophesy, and teach; the office is confirmed by signs and wonders. While some may claim that the office of apostle was only meant for the original twelve disciples, the biblical text extends this classification to others as well.

First and foremost is the Apostle Paul. Who could deny his calling and ability to function in the office of apostle? He along with Luke wrote much of our New Testament. He experienced beatings and torture; but is credited with taking the good news to the Gentile believers in spite of the harsh reality of persecutions he was forced to endure.

He preached the word, taught, and performed signs, wonders, and miracles; even to the point of raising the dead. Paul planted churches and established leadership (See 1 Co. 3:10). He was one of our greatest examples, short of Jesus.

He demonstrated a parental heart to lead, guide, and correct when necessary... those he was responsible for. He even held Peter responsible for hypocritical behavior when he separated himself from the Gentiles and would only eat with the Jews (See Galatians 2:11).

Do we still need apostles to take responsibility for planting new churches, working with the other four offices, raising up leadership in the church today? Of course, we do; and we will continue to need those called of God to function in the capacity of apostle until the day Jesus returns to take His bride. The first twelve apostles were not the only apostles, they were merely the first ones chosen by God.

The apostle cannot be appointed by man, and the office cannot be earned through service, study, acts or good deeds. Unlike the other offices, the Apostle is often able to perform any or all of the other four functions in the fivefold ministry. He or she has more authority than any of the other four offices and is the overseer of those people for which he is responsible.

Are there truly any modern-day Apostles some ask? In fact, as I teach on the gifts, I have heard that question on numerous occasions. While some may refer to themselves and/or others as apostles, how can a true apostle be identified?

We need look no further than the fruit. We know an apple tree by its fruit, a pear tree the same. We can identify an apostle by the fruit their ministry bears.

Working as a part of a worldwide ministry, I can tell you there are many that I work with, both directly and indirectly, that bear the fruit suggestive of apostleship. Few would tout this honor on their name badge, nevertheless the proof is in what they do for the kingdom.

In the book, *Understanding the Fivefold Ministry* edited by Matthew D. Green (Green, 2005), a number of different stories about modern day apostles are discussed. While many biblical scholars believe the offices of apostle and prophet are once again gaining recognition as active offices for the church, what do you say? Are there apostles in your midst?

Look around, do you see those that are busy planting churches, equipping the saints, advising other ministry leaders; do you see ministries that have experienced signs and wonders?

No one need tell you that they are called to this honor; but the signs that follow, and the fruit that they bear, are like bright neon signs confirming the call of God on their lives. There are indeed apostles in our midst.

The Prophet

For some the term prophet is associated with the prophets of old. Prophets like Samuel, Ezekiel, and Jeremiah who spoke the truth even when it wasn't convenient to do so.

Some would seem to think we no longer need the prophet in the body of Christ today. However, now more than ever before, we need the prophet to provide guidance and direction to the modern-day church.

The prophet is the second most important office within the body and is responsible for speaking the heart of God and foretelling future events. God does nothing except He tells His prophets first (Amos 3:7). The prophet is a teacher with a consistent manifestation of the revelation gifts plus prophecy.

Although we are urged in the scriptures to covet to prophesy, the gift of prophecy alone does not make one a prophet. The scriptures also tell us that all may prophesy, but we know not all are called to hold the office of a prophet.

Those who stand in the office of a prophet are once again those who are called and set apart for the office by Jesus. Unlike the gift of prophecy, they may be used to correct and admonish the body when needed. The prophet was and is a visionary called of God to function as a watchman and is responsible for speaking forth both God's will and His intentions.

We have biblical examples of both men and women who stood in the office of a prophet. It does not matter if they are a man or a woman, Greek or Jew; they must simply be called, chosen, and set aside to fulfill the office by God.

The evidence will become obvious as the fruit falls from the lips of those who speak. We can see in the word of God prophets who changed their environment both in the supernatural and the natural, as God led them.

Prophets receive their message from God in a variety of different ways including: visions, dreams, declarations, or through a knowing from within (the still small "voice," 1 Kings 19). The prophet may speak the word of the Lord, write it, or demonstrate it through the way they live their life.

A perfect example of this was Hosea whose life was a living parable. Other terms that may be used for prophet are seers or oracles of God, defining the nature of their ministry to the body.

Although proof of one's calling in this area will be confirmed by a fulfillment of their words, we must take care to remember that some prophecy is conditional based upon the hearer's response.

Take for an example the warning of Jonah the reluctant prophet, the warning he spoke was heeded and the people were spared.

Because of the corrective nature of some prophecies, the prophet will not always be welcomed with open arms. The true test of the prophet is that they are willing to suffer hardship to fulfill their calling and to deliver the word of the Lord to His people.

Who are some modern-day prophets of the church? There are many that may fall into this classification. Having lived on the west coast for six years, I had the opportunity to hear and see a few of them in person. Prophetically gifted ministers such as Shawn Bolz, Patricia King, and Bobby Connor spoke from time to time in a church I attended.

I had the opportunity to attend a wonderful conference with Jane Hamon. In fact, I am aware that there is a heavy prophetic influence from those involved with the ministry of Christian International in Florida, of which she and many others are a part.

Other well-known prophets who have recently gone on to their heavenly reward are Kim Clement, Bob Jones, and John Paul Jackson. The first two in particular, continue to have their prophecies come to fruition in the present time.

The Evangelist

The fivefold ministry office of the evangelist is filled by one called of God and who proclaims the good news to those who are outside of the kingdom of God, with a focus on bringing men and women to Christ. They may preach or teach the word. They usually do so with great passion, and with compassion for the lost.

They are well established in the word. The work that they do may include the working of signs, wonders, miracles, as well as deliverance. Their calling will be evidenced by the souls won through their ministry. They will lead new converts into baptism and direct them into a local body or start one if necessary.

They are not called to minister to one particular body of believers. The evangelist is usually one who travels to win the lost and is the one who breaks the ground for the work of the other ministries. He is the forerunner.

One of the greatest evangelists of our time is Billy Graham. Some reports suggest that more than 3.2 million people accepted the Lord as a result of his ministry. Another you may have heard of is Reinhard Bonnke.

One incident I read about was back in 2001 in Nigeria. A pastor there had a horrific accident and died. Two days later the pastor's wife, hearing that Bonnke was ministering nearby, had her husband's body taken to the location.

While Bonnke ministered to the crowd, the dead body was being closely guarded in another room. Soon the body began to twitch, the dead pastor regained consciousness, opened his eyes, and sat up. Unaware of what had taken place in the other room, Bonnke left the building and boarded a plane. He later learned of the miracle that had transpired while he ministered to others during the crusade.

Signs and wonders will follow those who believe, even when the ministering evangelist is unaware of the miracle taking place. Many may evangelize, even in the streets, but not all are members of the fivefold ministry office of evangelist.

The Pastor

The Greek word for pastor is "poiman", meaning shepherd. We typically think of the shepherd as carrying the rod and staff to lead, guide, direct or correct the sheep. They shepherd the sheep of God's flock. He or she is called to tend, teach, protect, correct, and feed them.

Those called to pastor the flock are to do so with a sincere heart. They display compassion for those they are called to lead. They will willingly lay down their own personal need to care for those they are called to minister to. They will serve the flock in many different capacities including but not limited to visitation, prayer, preaching, teaching, ministering to the sick and the widows, and watching out for those who might want to do harm to God's flock.

Their responsibilities are diverse, but first and foremost, they must be given to study and prayer. They lead by example through a spirit filled life. They do not <u>drive</u> the sheep, but gently guide them.

They are not to dictate or take advantage of the flock; but rather to lay down their own personal agendas for the needs of those they oversee. They must be committed and loyal, humbling themselves to become a servant, even as Jesus did.

Although they are responsible for the care of the sheep, they must not neglect their personal growth and relationship with the Lord. The pastor's first responsibility is to the Lord, not to the sheep. The true pastor exalts the Lord Jesus Christ and not himself. These qualities may also apply to anyone called as an elder.

Pastors of growing churches must pay close attention to their own limitations and learn to engage in delegation of responsibilities as is appropriate. The early disciples found themselves buried in managing the care of the widows, to the extent that it was hindering their ability to study and pray. Therefore, they had to choose others to oversee the work. Godly men of good reputation were released to minister to the widows, freeing the apostles to devote themselves to their other responsibilities.

Tommy Barnett wrote, "the pastor must begin to view his role not only as a shepherd but also as a rancher." (Barnett, 2004) He notes that the modern-day pastor must be open to finding ways to minister to an ever expanding and diverse grouping of people.

Their needs are as diverse as the people. Pastors need to engage the assistance of under shepherds to shoulder a portion of the burden for the care of the varying groups. He goes on to say of the pastor, "As a rancher, he helps set the direction for all these shepherds so

the entire flock can embrace a like vision and operate in unity."
(Barnett, 2004)

Here we see the importance of a shared vision in creating unity in
the body. The pastor's ability to communicate the vision and
engage the congregation in fulfilling the vision, is crucial to
creating unity within the church.

It is becoming increasingly more important for the pastor to
develop an expanded vision reaching beyond his or her own local
body. This expanded vision may include joining other ministries in
projects that reach out into the community and the world beyond.
My own church recently participated by hosting the Tim Tebow,
"Night to Shine" project. Many different organizations beyond our
own were required to effectively minister to the disabled in this
eventful night. We also actively send missionaries and support
missionaries in various locations all around the world.

The very large church I was a part of in California just before I
moved, has an annual community weekend. The church cancels
services in its numerous locations and schedules community
projects for the whole weekend. They paint schools, rebuild
playgrounds, do landscaping in the parks and other community
areas, all in cooperation with local authorities.

Another church that I have had the opportunity to minister in over
the past 6 years, has been growing in their community outreach.
When I first met them, the church was just beginning to do
community ministry. Over the years their impact in their
community and city has grown exponentially.

They do weekly community meals, give away food, plant gardens,
provide minor house repairs and landscaping to the poor and
disabled. They adopted a school and are actively supporting the
school and its staff. They express the love of God to their
community by their good deeds, their active presence in
community events, and educational opportunities.

The pastor's vision can no longer be limited to how can he/she care for the sheep. The vision must grow to how can I and the sheep of my pasture make an impact for good in our community, our city, and the world beyond.

The Teacher

The fifth and final gift we want to explore is the gift of the teacher. The teacher expounds, exhorts, explains, and teaches the word of the Lord to believers, to strengthen their faith and understanding of the gospel. They teach doctrine, ethics, reverence, history, and the timeline for events that are found within the pages of our bible.

The teacher helps to mature the body by teaching the basic beliefs and doctrines laid out in our scripture and explaining how to apply those principals to one's life.

They take even the most intricate and deep precepts and make them accessible to those they teach. They have a knack for taking what seems difficult to comprehend and opening it up for all to understand. While the teacher is especially gifted in the ability to explain biblical truths, all elders should be willing to teach both in word and deed.

I remember many years ago, I was called out and given a prophetic word. I was a new Christian at the time and had no idea what God's calling was for my life. The woman spoke of a tall set of baking shelves with cookies on each level.

She said, you will have the ability to pull the cookies off of the top shelf and place them on the bottom shelf so that all can partake. She went on to explain that she was referring to the deeper things of God. She said you will be able to take complicated spiritual principles and make them plain for all to see and understand. An interesting word for one who had not even taught one bible class, not even to the children.

While the office of teacher is a specific gifting within the fivefold team, all members of the fivefold ministry are expected to teach those that they lead.

Are all called to be members of the fivefold ministry team? Not at all, it is a team chosen and ordained by God. If every member were a leader, who would follow? However, every member of the body is important; and as Jesus reminded us, those called to leadership are there to serve others.

Final Thoughts on the Five

Christ came to build a body of related believers. He left us with a gift to administrate the process under His authority. The gift? The fivefold ministry was left to put things in order, to equip and empower the body for the work of the ministry.

> *[13] Till we all come in the unity of the faith, and of the knowledge of the Son of God, unto a perfect man, unto the measure of the stature of the fulness of Christ:*
>
> *[14] That we henceforth be no more children, tossed to and fro, and carried about with every wind of doctrine, by the sleight of men, and cunning craftiness, whereby they lie in wait to deceive;*
>
> *[15] But speaking the truth in love, may grow up into him in all things, which is the head, even Christ:*
>
> *[16] From whom the whole body fitly joined together and compacted by that which every joint supplieth, according to the effectual working in the measure of every part, maketh increase of the body unto the edifying of itself in love. Ephesians 4:13-16*

The fivefold ministry is the power team, the construction workers, the body building personal trainers of the church. They shoulder the responsibility of administrative duties within the body of believers.

For many years, the church has functioned with more of a threefold style leadership, rather than the fivefold model that God had intended. While pastors, teachers, and evangelists have been the accepted norm, many are seeing a restoration of the fivefold model taking place.

There are two other gifts sets that are crucial to individual believers and the body. In the next chapter, we will explore the gifts of the Spirit. These are the gifts that equip us with the tools to minister to one another and meet the needs of the body.

Where does this ministry take place you may ask? We minister to one another with our gifts in the relationships we form with one another. Healthy relationships with one another are key to the overall health of the church. I know that I have said it before, but it bears repeating. We need each other.

Chapter Six:

The Power Tools of Ministry

I recently purchased a condominium in Michigan. While much had already been done to update my new home, there was still much to do. I wanted to make it uniquely my own. Things like adding ceiling fans, changing the color of the cabinets, hanging a pot rack on the wall. Why I even decided to work on the unfinished basement to make it livable for a second home office.

I was able to do small things like laying a new floor in the bathrooms. However, items that required special expertise and power tools specifically, would call for a skilled electrician and handyman. While tools such as hammers, screwdrivers, and hand saws may be adequate for small things, other projects require more powerful tools.

As we do life together, our relationships with other believers afford us the opportunity to use our gifts to build up one another. We have tools such as compassion, understanding, caring, and even prayer that we can utilize. However, spirit-filled Christians have added to their arsenal, the power tools of the Spirit. Spiritual gifts give us powerful and effective tools with which to build up the body of believers, the church.

> *but speaking the truth in love, we are to grow up in all aspects into Him who is the head, even Christ, from whom the whole body being fitted and held together by what every joint supplies, according to the proper working of each individual part, causes the growth of the body for the building up of itself in love. Ephesians 4:15*

Growing and maturing in love toward one another is key. Our relationships with God and one another empower us to grow up and fulfill our God given destiny. It is in those relationships that we meet the needs of others through the use of our gifts.

We will address motivational gifts in the next chapter, but here we will explore spiritual gifts. What are they, where do they come from, and how shall we use them to meet the needs of our brothers and sisters in the Lord? Let us begin by reviewing this scripture.

> *"Now there are varieties of gifts, but the same Spirit. [5] And there are varieties of ministries, and the same Lord. [6] There are varieties of effects, but the same God who works all things in all persons." 1 Corinthians 12:4-6*

Now there are diversities of gifts but the same Spirit.

Let us examine the root meanings of the word gifts in the Greek, which is charisma.

- chara = joy

- charis = grace in the abstract

- charisma = grace (God's power) made available in a specific and personal way. It empowers the one who possesses it.[3]

The gifts of Holy Spirit empower believers for the work of the ministry. They give us Holy Ghost power to perform actions that are not possible on our own in the natural. Allow me to illustrate.

Let us say that you have grass that is growing higher and higher. Going out with scissors to cut the blades of grass is time consuming and ineffective, they are not the tool of choice. So, you buy a lawn mower. The lawn mower is a more effective means of accomplishing this task. However, unless you have a source of fuel such as gasoline or electricity, that lawnmower will do nothing but sit there. It cannot cut one blade of grass without a supply of power.

---

[3] Refer to your Strong's Concordance for more information.

Within the body of Christ there are needs to be met. We are not a complete body on our own, we need each other and the gifts each has been endowed with to fully provide for one another. In 1 Corinthians 12:11 it tells us the Holy Spirit "distributing to each one individually just as He wills." Further in the KJV it says, "*He divides severally as He wills.*"

This tells us that we each have been given several gifts by the determination of Holy Spirit to use in the work of the ministry. Because none of us possess all of the gifts, we need each other. Together we are fully empowered to meet every need.

Those in search of answers to a dilemma, may find a person with the gift of a "word of wisdom" helpful in identifying a solution. The person who is sick, will find one with a gift of healing beneficial to the restoration of their health. Others may be ministered to through the gift of miracles or faith.

How many gifts are there? There are probably too many to cover in this book, however Paul has identified a list of nine. This is by no means an exhaustive list, and many bible scholars have compiled their own list of gifts, and even their own gift tests. C. Peter Wagner, a well-known bible theologian who has gone on to his heavenly reward, identified twenty-one gifts. Others have compiled other lists of gifts.

For the sake of clarity, we will address the nine identified by the Apostle Paul in 1 Corinthians 12:7:11:

> *But to each one is given the manifestation of the Spirit for the common good. [8]For to one is given the word of wisdom through the Spirit, and to another the word of knowledge according to the same Spirit [9]to another faith by the same Spirit, and to another gifts of healing by the one Spirit, [10]and to another the effecting of miracles, and to another prophecy, and to another the distinguishing of spirits, to another various kinds of tongues, and to another the interpretation of*

tongues. [11]But one and the same Spirit works all these things, distributing to each one individually just as He wills.

Spiritual, Manifestation or Sign Gifts

The manifestation gifts are gifts given to us by the Holy Spirit and they may be imparted by the laying on of hands. They are, as the name implies, a manifestation of the Spirit.

Some refer to these gifts as the sign gifts, perhaps in light of the fact that they are a demonstration or sign to all that witness them in operation. They are frequently divided into three groups of three. It is interesting to note that the number three is the number of divine perfection.

There are three gifts of revelation, three gifts of power, and three gifts of inspiration or utterance. Let us examine the three classifications and the gifts they each include.

The Gifts of Revelation

- discerning of spirits
- word of wisdom
- word of knowledge

The Gifts of Power

- faith
- gifts of healing
- miracles

The Gifts of Inspiration

- prophecy
- Gift of tongues
- interpretation of tongues

The bible is full of the supernatural acts and works of God. It is impossible to read the New Testament and not notice incident after incident of the miraculous; first of all, through the hands of Jesus in the gospels. Even after His ascension, the acts continued to be performed by His disciples.

Paul, during his long ministry in Ephesus, had many signs and wonders following his ministry. In Acts 19:11 we see an account where "special miracles" were accomplished through the hands of Paul. The word "special" in this case meaning they were not the ordinary types of miracles, not that any miracles are normal. The word miracle itself sets the event apart from what is considered the norm of the day. These particular miracles were more miraculous than the signs that had been witnessed prior to this incident.

As we search for reasons these miraculous incidents took place, we can see that it had a definite connection to the preaching of the gospel of the Kingdom. First of all, it was a sign to attract people to hear the gospel, and secondly to authenticate the ministry. This is how we get the term "sign gifts".

An investigation of the Christians of the New Testament reveals that the people of that era were not unlike Christians of the present day. They knew sorrow and joy, riches and poverty, strength and weakness, health and sickness, and yet everywhere they went supernatural power and the miraculous manifested.

What exactly did they do in their meetings and churches? They were praying (Acts 6:5-6), preaching (Acts 8:12), they sang hymns and spiritual songs, and psalms, (Colossians 3:16), they partook in the Lord's Supper (Matt.26:26-30), took up collections (1 Corinthians 16:1-2), they fasted (Acts 13:2). Their meetings were not unlike ours; they were open to Holy Spirit and experienced the supernatural manifestation of His presence.

These people had vivid experiences with Holy Spirit. They knew when, where, and how He came. This is evidenced by Paul when he asked them in Acts 19:2 if they had experienced Him since they believed.

Those who were baptized in the Spirit spoke in tongues and prophesied. This shows an obvious connection between the baptism of the Spirit and the gifts of the Spirit. The word manifestation in the Greek (phanerosis)[4] means coming to light or revealing. The Holy Spirit reveals God shining through us as we exercise His gifts.

The supernatural should be an everyday experience; this includes the operation of the gifts. As we seek Him with a sense of expectation, a manifestation of His Spirit and His gifts should be commonplace. Afterall, we are partakers of the divine nature of Christ.

When earnestly studying the gifts, there are three chapters in 1 Corinthians that are most notable. They are chapters twelve, thirteen, and fourteen. Chapter twelve lists the gifts and the different administrations, but that it is the same Spirit; it is the power chapter. Chapter fourteen is the love chapter and how to use the gifts in love.

Chapter thirteen is the integral link between the two chapters explaining what the gifts are like when they are not used in love, in comparison to when they are used in love. These three chapters relate perfectly to scripture found in 2 Timothy 1:7 which tells us that *"We have not received the spirit of fear but of power, and of love, and of a sound mind."*

The words "is given" in 1 Corinthians 12:7 is the word "Didotai" in the Greek. This simply means that it is not just given one time but is continually being given. It is not about our ability but about our availability. Therefore, none of us needs to fear that we cannot or will not be used, for Holy Spirit gives us the gifts that empower us to minister to the body.

---

[4] See Strong's 5321

We all have something from Holy Spirit to contribute. We must always remember that the gifts are to be used properly and in order (1 Corinthians 14:33). There is to be an order maintained within the service as the Lord is not the author of confusion. Therefore, we must be mindful of the protocol to be utilized in accordance with our scriptures and in accordance with the governing offices of the local body.

Let us begin with the three Gifts of Revelation which give us the power to know.

Gifts of Revelation

Word of Wisdom

The word of wisdom is the supernatural revelation of divine purpose. It is not wisdom in and of itself, but it is a word of wisdom. This implies that it is not complete but merely a portion or measure of the wisdom which we receive. God is all knowing so whatever portion He chooses to reveal to His servants; it is a portion of the full wisdom of God.

It may foretell the future and is one of the greatest of the revelatory gifts. It is not to be confused with the gift of prophecy which is not foretelling in nature. Prophets are also known as seers and they speak of the future as a result of the gift of the word of wisdom.

Word of Knowledge

The word of knowledge is a supernatural revelation of facts that can only be revealed through the disclosure of Holy Spirit. For instance, when Jesus spoke to the woman at the well, He spoke to her of facts He could not have known except they were revealed to Him by the divine mind of God.

I can tell you of one instance where the Lord used me to minister to a woman who had been making statements contrary to the Lord's word for her life. I had never heard her make these statements, but I heard them roll over and over again in my mind like a broken record.

Finally, I approached her and asked if I could pray with her. She was quite receptive, so I began to pray. I found myself repeating those same words to her with a message that she was not to say them anymore.

There was then a divine explanation through the exercising of the word of wisdom explaining to her why what she had said was not true. The woman was quite amazed as she knew that I could not have heard the conversation that I repeated to her. She knew that the message had to be divinely inspired as I could have had no knowledge of the situation.

The Discerning of Spirits

This is a supernatural revelation into the realm of the spirit to know what spirit is in operation whether it is a good spirit or a bad spirit. A good example can be found in Acts 13: 9-10 when Paul spoke to Elymas the sorcerer.

That will complete our discourse of the gifts of revelation. The second set of the three spiritual gifts of manifestation are the gifts of power.

Gifts of Power

Faith

This is the supernatural belief in the power of God for the impossible to happen. This is not to be confused with the measure of faith that we each receive. (Romans 12:3) No, the gift of faith is related to the ability to believe God for supernatural happenings.

It is not the same kind of faith we need to believe for salvation. It is not the faith we need to believe God to fulfill His word. This is a far greater gift as it moves the bearer into the realm of believing for the unbelievable and the ability to rest in that knowledge of supernatural provision, protection, and healing.

A Supernatural Provision

I know of a lady who had lost her job and her unemployment had been held up. She was given a ticket to visit relatives over the Christmas vacation. In spite of the fact that she had no viable income to support her for the trip, she went.

While away, she received an invitation to an important conference. She had no income, no sign of income in the near future, and bills mounting higher and higher… it seemed ridiculous to even take the invitation seriously. In fact, an acquaintance hearing of the invitation, scolded her for even thinking about it at all.

Nevertheless, she could not shake the feeling that she was to go. So, she simply laid it out before the Lord and said, "Lord, if you want me to go you will have to provide the funds." Once again, the situation from all angles was simply impossible; yet she found herself believing that God would make a way for her.

Within three days, three weeks' worth of unemployment was deposited into her account. Then a check arrived, more than enough to cover the trip. Finally, she got a phone call from an employer who wanted to start her on orientation for a job that was to only be for one day a week. It hardly seemed worth the trouble, but she went anyway. When she got there, they told her that she was to work full time for 3 -4 weeks to fulfill her orientation.

Within four weeks she had several thousand dollars in the bank and another $3000 that would arrive before she was to leave to take the trip. Her bills were paid, her trip was paid. She had more than enough to pay for everything, and still had money left over.

Do you know what put the icing on the cake for her? When she got to the location of the meeting and went to rent her car, the agent at the desk took one look at her license and said, "Today is your birthday?" She said yes. Then the agent said to her, "Do you mind if I give you a free upgrade?" Then she pointed to the car sitting outside on the curb, it was a Sebring convertible.

The lady drove away in the car in total disbelief. She phoned her friend and said, "You are not going to believe what just happened to me!" You see, that is the kind of God we serve. He is a "more than enough" kind of God.

The Working of Miracles

This is the supernatural intervention and power of God in the course of nature. The first example that comes to mind is the parting of the Red Sea. That was nothing short of a miracle. Of course, there are many others, but that one stands out to me first and foremost. There are some who would argue that God did miracles in bible days, but not in present times.

Once again, I know of a lady who was driving home from work one night. She was working as a nurse in a nursing home on the second shift. One of the patients had become extremely confused that night and had begged her to stay. The nurse knew he was prone to spells of confusion, so she thought nothing of it.

She got into her car to drive the 30 miles to home and turned on the radio. About halfway home she was on top of a hill and descending down the other side when the radio began to fade, so she reached over to adjust the station. As she did, the car was suddenly propelled forward at a rapid rate of speed and began to spin about in the opposite direction.

She did not understand what was happening at first, but found the car rolling in midair as the other car, the car that had hit her from behind, was pulling away. She was not wearing a seatbelt, so the impact threw her about violently inside the car. She broke the mirror with her forehead; bent the steering wheel with her chest, and her knee broke the knob off of the stick shift.

As the car finally landed, by the grace of God on all four wheels, she found herself surrounded by tall corn on four sides. The only thing she said as she rolled high above the corn was to cry out to God for help. There was little time for anything else.

Now she somehow survived the crash and the violent ascent and descent from midair into a field of corn. She was so deep into the field, that she had no idea which direction the road might be. The full-grown corn surrounding her, was still standing.

She found herself asking the Lord for help once more. You see the crash had thrown her so high in the air that the corn around her had not been touched. The doors were jammed shut from the crash, and the windows were all cracked, and only the driver's side window was broken out enough for her to attempt to climb out, and that had sharp jagged points protruding from the edge.

Fearing the crash and the field of corn may cause the car to suddenly burst into flames, she determined she must get out of the car at all costs. She asked the Lord for help and pulled her legs up into the seat. She had no idea how she was going to pull herself out of the window without getting seriously hurt.

The jagged points of glass would probably slice her, but she did not care. She just wanted out. So, as she began to poke her head out of the top portion of the window, she suddenly found herself some 35 feet away from the car and outside of the field trying to catch her balance in the ditch.

How did she get there? She did not know. One moment she was climbing out the window and the next she was standing alongside the road. She knew that she had never finished climbing through the window. She knows that she did not determine a direction to go to walk toward the road. She was baffled, how was this possible? She did not climb out of the car or walk to the edge of the road, under her own power.

A lady who had observed the crash returned to say, "I thought you were dead; so, I chased the car that hit you! He pulled away from me in excess of 120 mph." The doctors and nurses that treated her at the hospital were all amazed.

They told her that she should have been dead, or at least critically hurt. Yet there was not one broken bone. There were no cuts deep enough to require a stitch. They did not even attempt to take any x-rays. They did not know what to x-ray.

The doctors, nurses, and state highway patrol were left scratching their heads. How could such a miracle have happened? I know how. It was an act of God. Miracles still happen, even today. They happen to ordinary people like you and like me. God is a very good God.

Gifts of Healing

This is the supernatural ability of God to heal diseases. You will notice that this gift is plural; it is the gifts of healing not the gift of healing. How many gifts are there? I'm not certain anyone even knows. We know there are many different kinds of sickness and the Lord is able to heal them all.

Gifts of Inspiration

These gifts give the bearers the ability to speak.

Prophecy

This is a supernatural inspiration to give a message in a known tongue. The gift of prophecy is for edification, exhortation, and comfort. To edify means to build up; to encourage the church.

To exhort simply means to encourage one another. It is not foretelling of the future. The bible tells us that we are to covet to prophesy. It also tells us that all may prophesy (1 Corinthians 14:31). Why? Because by doing so we build, encourage, and comfort one another.

An example of a prophecy might be the following:

> *"The Lord says, 'I love you with an everlasting love. I will never leave you nor forsake you. I see what you are going through. Do not fear for I am God and I am right beside you holding your hand. Nothing can harm you for you are my child and I take care of all that are mine. If I know the*

number of hairs on your head, then I certainly know what it is you are facing, and you need not be afraid for I am with you always. The Lord is a good God and He gives good gifts to His children. You are blessed with my favor but more importantly you have my love.'"

This is the gift that Phillip's four daughters had, they could exhort and comfort. They could not foretell the future because they were not called to the office of a prophet (1 Corinthians 14:3).

John Eckhardt in his book, "God Still Speaks" said, "We encourage believers who are not called into the office of a prophet to stay within the limit of edification, exhortation, and comfort. Prophets are the ones who have the authority to speak beyond the limit of edification, exhortation, and comfort." (Eckhardt, 2009)

The gift is subject to the one using it, that means they can control it and must know when, where, and how to do so. One must know how to prophesy in accordance with the regulations and order set forth in the body of believers they are in. In 1 Corinthians 14:29 it tells us to let two or three speak and let the others judge.

Some churches ask that a word be shared with a leader first to gain permission to release it to the congregation. It is important to know what the rules are so that you may use your gift decently and in order. Once again, God is not the author of confusion. Knowing when, where, and how to release a word of prophecy comes with experience.

Diverse Kinds of Tongues

This is the supernatural ability to speak in an unknown tongue. It is not to be confused with one's prayer language. We know that on the day of Pentecost the Holy Spirit was given and they began to speak in tongues. That is not the sign gift of tongues.

The sign gift is the divine ability to give a message in tongues that will then require an interpretation. If one gives a message in tongues and there is no one there to interpret it, then the one giving the message should be able to interpret it or remain silent.

Interpretation of Tongues

This is the divine supernatural ability to give the interpretation of a message in tongues. Holy Spirit reveals the meaning to the bearer of this gift. It is not a word for word translation, but rather an interpretation of the message given.

All of these gifts are supernatural and require faith to bring them into operation.

Chapter Seven:

The Power of Uniqueness

I tried out for the senior class play in high school. I had played the main part in the one-act play competition two years running so I had my heart set on one of the main characters in this play. Besides, I had less competition for this play because only people in the senior class could audition.

They began the tryouts with the smaller parts first. Not wanting to put all my eggs in one basket, I decided it would be best to try out for all the female characters. The experience of reading for the smaller parts would help me prepare to read for the bigger roles, or so I thought. Then if I did not get one of the major parts, I would still have the opportunity to take one of the lesser parts instead. I thought a small part was better than no part.

I did not anticipate what happened next. Once I read for the first part, they gave it to me. They stopped the auditions; no one else even had an opportunity to try out. My fate was sealed with the first reading. Who would have imagined something like that would have happened? I certainly didn't.

I tried to convince the directors to let me read for the other parts, but they refused. They said that I was perfect for *this* part, and *this* part was perfect for me, and no one else would do. Of all the things that I would *not* want to be this had to be at the top of my list, a gypsy fortune teller? You have got to be kidding. Nevertheless, it was the role I was forced to play in this drama. That was many years ago.

Our Gift Motivates Us

Why is it important to operate in one's own specific motivational gift? The cast has been set, and the parts have been awarded. Each of us has a specific role or part to play in the body of Christ. I can't do Mary's part and Mary can't do mine. Why? Because each of us was created with the specific gifts and talents needed to fulfill our purpose. No one else will do quite like you.

Paul was referring to the uniqueness of each individual in the body and the significance of their gift to the body when he wrote, "And the eye cannot say to the hand, 'I have no need of you'; or again the head to the feet, 'I have no need of you.'" 1 Corinthians 12:21

The motivational gift is defined as a spiritual endowment, a gift of grace. The gift is a lifestyle or personality gift. It is not something that can be earned. Just as there are varieties of gifts there are also varieties of ministries and varieties of effects. We each have the one gift, the motivational gift with which to minister to one another in the body.

The motivational gift is referred to as one's personality or lifestyle gift. It makes us who we are in terms of our personality, and it motivates us to act or react based upon that gift. It is fundamental to who we are or at least to who we are to become, if we cooperate with God. It is a gift from God the Father.

You might be questioning the biblical basis to support this concept; I am so glad you asked the question!

> *There are varieties of effects, but the same God who works all things in all persons. 1 Corinthians 12:6*

The KJV uses the word "operations" instead of effects. We operate in ministry through our motivational gift. The parable of Jesus regarding the pounds actually relates to the motivational gifts.

> *And he called ten of his slaves, and gave them minas (pounds) and said to them, 'Do business [with this] until I come [back]. Luke 19:13*

We are to go into the entire world and preach the gospel. We are to make disciples. That is our business. We have been commissioned by God himself to take what He has given to us and do business with it until He returns.

You will notice that unlike the parable of the talents, in this parable he gave only one pound to each person. There were ten pounds and ten servants, one apiece.

As we look deeply at this passage, it becomes clear that Jesus is not speaking about the spiritual gifts, because the Holy Spirit can give out several gifts or manifestations to each person, not just one. We also know that this parable cannot refer directly to the five-fold ministry gift. Some are called to fulfill that ministry in the church but not all.

Therefore, the only gift set left to consider in this parable is the motivational gift given by the Father. In scripture, there are only seven motivational gifts, we each only have one that is dominant. Jesus was the only one that operated in all seven in their fullness. He was complete and perfect.

What did Jesus instruct us to do? Occupy, and utilize the gift you were given to do the work of the ministry, to overthrow the kingdom of Satan in people's lives and establish the kingdom of Heaven.

> *As each one has received a special gift, employ it in serving one another as good stewards of the manifold grace of God. Whoever speaks, is to do so as one who is speaking the utterances of God; whoever serves is to do so as one who is serving by the strength which God supplies; so that in all things God may be glorified through Jesus Christ, to whom belongs the glory and dominion forever and ever. Amen. 1 Peter 4:10-11*

The motivational gift is usually something we think of as a personality gift we were born with, but it is generally understood that it is not sanctified for the Father's use until we have been born again. The word sanctified means to be "holy or set apart".

If you look at the word motivate, it consists of two root words in combination; the words motion and action. Therefore, it is our motivational gift that causes us to move and act in the way that we do. There are three forms of motivation. They are:

1. Fear

2. Reward or incentive

3. Attitude or character

Motivation is the energizing power and nature that urges us to move in specific ways.

For instance, one of my children was a real "book worm" as we used to say. Even as a toddler he loved his books. While other children were playing with their trucks, cars, and trains, he could be found sitting in a quiet corner reading his books.

This was more than a passing infatuation. As he grew and matured, this fascination followed him. He was an excellent student, and even as an adult he found that writing and reading books was just a part of who he was. His inborn personality motivated him to act and react in predictable ways. He continues to develop the gift.

Classifications of Motivational Gifts

While you will not find a motivational gift for writing books, the tendencies can be found within the more generalized classifications. Paul outlines a list of seven different grace or motivational gifts. They are prophecy, serving, teaching, exhortation, giving, administration, and mercy. Remember that the word gift in the Greek is charisma; and the root of that is chara. Chara means joy.

People who have a talent for writing may use it to exercise the motivational gifts of prophesy, teaching, or exhortation. Whatever your gifts and talents may be, they make up who you are collectively. When we recognize our gifts of grace and minister through those gifts, we minister with joy. A sense of fulfillment and satisfaction can only be fully realized as we learn to function in our place within the gifts of grace that God has given us.

We each have one gift that is more dominant than the rest. However, we should have portions of all seven classifications. Jesus who was perfect, had all seven. He did not have them in varying measures, but in full measure.

As individuals, we cannot attain this perfection without one another. We each have a measure or part which does not become complete except when we are joined together in Him. We may have several that are more profound from the others, but there will be one that is the most dominant.

Let us examine the seven classifications as outlined by the Apostle Paul.

The Motivational Gift of Prophecy

People with the dominant gift of prophecy may have very strong opinions about right and wrong. Peter is one who exhibited many of the following tendencies. Remember, these are merely tendencies often seen in people with this gift, but not necessarily a rule.

The person with this dominant motivational gift understands the heart of God and wishes to defend it openly. They possess a strong, uncompromising personality and can seem difficult to get along with, holding hard to established rules and laws. Their thoughts and beliefs are unwavering.

It is important for the prophetically motivated person to learn how to speak the truth in love, with compassion. This is often something they will have to develop.

Characteristics may also include:

- no tolerance for others' mistakes and they may find it difficult to forgive

- make snap judgments and are quick to correct and criticize others

- express strong feelings and opinions

- iron clad opinion of right

- intuitive sense regarding how God sees things

- desire quick action regarding wrongs done and tend to reject the person as a warning to others.

- tenacious in their beliefs

- they are like bull dogs; holding fast to the stand they take

- persuasive in defining right from wrong and desire to see repentance and change

- they are very broken when they fail

- narrow and short sighted, must work to remain open minded

- ability to discern good from evil

- their overwhelming boldness can frighten others

Peter is a striking example of just such a person. He was head strong and opinionated but loyal; he was eager to prove his commitment to Jesus. Therefore, when he denied Jesus the night he was arrested, he became distraught.

Once he overcame the brokenness, he was one of the strongest allies in the cause to fulfill the Great Commission. His out-spokenness was used for good on the day of Pentecost, resulting in many accepting the Lord. They are willing to suffer for doing right because they are so deeply committed to the cause of justice and truth.

It is important to be aware of the negative tendencies, but not become discouraged by them. When we understand this as a motivational grace from God, we can work to overcome any apparent weakness and use it as a strength.

If I want a loyal follower that I can trust to watch my back, the person with this gift who has committed themselves to my cause would be an ideal candidate. Once they have made up their mind to support a person or cause, they will be hard pressed to turn back.

Because of the tendencies mentioned here, they are easily misunderstood and thought to be too harsh and frank. Others may view them as unyielding, headstrong, unfriendly, rude, and even manipulative.

Remember, without submission to the Holy Spirit these traits can all become very real. Walking in love and operating in the fruit of the Spirit are extremely crucial, and required by the Lord, irrespective of one's gifting.

One of their most striking qualities is the ability to discern good from evil, all the while exposing and confronting the evil. This is necessary to protect the church from those who wish to deceive. They are persuasive, authoritative, and courageous. Once again, this can be used to unite or divide depending upon how one uses their gift.

Having the motivational gift of prophecy does not make one a prophet, nor does it ensure that they will have the spiritual gift of prophecy. Each of these gifts operates independently of one another.

Others in the bible with this gift include Elijah, Jeremiah, John the Baptist, Isaiah, and Jonah, of course all of these are clearly prophets as well.

The Motivational Gift of Serving

The person with this dominant motivational gift can be a great asset to the church and a loyal helper. They genuinely enjoy taking care of the practical needs of others and seek opportunities to do so, often doing more than what is expected or even needed at times.

They enjoy doing manual labor and will work on their own if need be to see a task completed. They enjoy working toward short term goals and prefer smaller projects, where quick results can be seen. They may even use their own funds to see a project completed rather than wait to obtain the necessary funds through the appropriate channels. They like their instructions spelled out in detail.

The servant's heart has a deep need to be accepted, needed, and verbally affirmed by those they serve. They often feel inadequate or unqualified for leadership roles. They are sincere, caring, and loving people. They are hospitable and generous.

They do not like to delegate work to others, creating the opportunity to become overworked. They are highly energetic and tend toward perfectionism. They are meticulous and dislike clutter. Their enthusiasm and high standards can cause others to feel intimidated. When they fail to walk in the Spirit, they can become vulnerable to:

- Overwork
- Self-pity
- Having a judgmental attitude
- Lack of direction
- Withdrawn
- Hurt
- Feeling unappreciated
- May be pushy in their desire to help others
- Can neglect family needs to meet needs of others

They do well as ushers, greeters, and on the hospitality committee. They are dedicated, sincere, and loyal people. They see life as a series of activities and their orientation is toward others.

Biblical examples can be found in Martha, Phoebe, Stephen, and Timothy.

The Motivational Gift of Teaching

Teachers love books, bookstores, research, maps, atlases, etc., and enjoy systematic, logical, and sequential presentation of the facts. They love word studies and using research books such as concordances and dictionaries and insist on accuracy. Their preoccupation with details and facts may make them seem insensitive.

Teachers prefer teaching believers rather than doing evangelism. They are more objective than subjective. They prefer illustrations that are taken directly from the bible rather than from life experiences and are very self-disciplined. They have a select group of friends and are emotionally self-controlled.

Their objectivity may make them seem cold and unfeeling. They enjoy using the Word to solve problems and they utilize an analytical approach to the truth. They are intellectually sharp and tend to develop a large vocabulary. This can lead to pride if they do not monitor it and walk in humility.

They tend to focus on accuracy and truth and will have to investigate the works of others before accepting their teaching.

The teacher is vulnerable to being:

- Insensitive

- Proud and critical

- Impatient

- Wordy

- Dogmatic

- Inconsistent

- Impractical

Teachers can run the risk of becoming so fact oriented that they fail to focus on the application of the truth in their lives. They may neglect the needs of those they serve in favor of time to spend studying. They may become so dependent upon their study skills that they discredit the ability of the Holy Spirit to bring illumination and revelation in the Word.

Once again, it becomes crucial that one know the areas in which they are vulnerable and take measures to prevent falling into those areas by remaining intimate with Holy Spirit on a daily basis.

Biblical examples of teachers are Ezra, Apollos, Luke, and Priscilla

The Motivational Gift of Exhortation

Those that have this gift are both motivators and encouragers. They encourage others to enjoy an abundant life. They are very optimistic and loving and tend to look on the positive side even in adverse situations. They like to stimulate the faith of others so that they can reach their full potential in Christ.

They can usually discern where people are spiritually and can minister to them at that level. They like to map out practical steps to help people grow and have no problem working with diverse groups of people. In fact, they like to encourage unity in believers from diverse groups.

They tend to view their trials and troubles as opportunities in which they can grow. They love people and enjoy helping them grow and mature. They are very patient and caring people; they do not give up easily. They usually make excellent counselors.

They prefer beginning with an experience and applying the Word to meet personal and practical needs. They take a biblical truth embedded in experience to help the listener understand and apply it to their personal life. Their positive attitude may seem unrealistic and others may think they are overly confident and independent.

Exhorters may become vulnerable to:

- Simplification
- Rationalizing
- Presumption
- Legalism
- Independence
- Overconfidence

Biblical examples of exhorters are Barnabus and Paul.

The Motivational Gift of Giving

This believer has a giving heart and a giving spirit. They are willing to share their own money, material wealth, spiritual blessings, and personal time with others.

They have a knack for knowing how to make and manage their finances. They usually live well under their means and tend to be wealthy. Their wisdom regarding making and investing money far exceeds the everyday experience; it extends into divine purpose.

The giver likes others to invest in the kingdom and they are keenly aware of the financial needs of others. They are self-motivated in giving to meet needs and they need no encouragement to do so. They prefer to give anonymously. They like it when their giving is an answer to someone else's prayer. They prefer to give in response to God's direct nudging and not in response to an appeal.

I worked for someone once who had this gift. In fact, they were exercising the gift at a fairly young age. When I met him, it was in response to an open position in the nursing home he owned. He purchased the home at the tender age of thirty-two. Even as a young man he was very wise with money and knew how to make it.

He went on to build an assisted living facility and later a very large Christian radio station. He was a fine Christian man who simply had the gift of giving and the wealth to prove it. Some people simply have this gift. He loved to give back to those he knew and loved; to his community, church, and to God's work. God knows the ones He can trust to distribute His wealth.

Those with this gift are vulnerable to:

- Using money to control others
- Using money to control the church
- Overemphasis on material things
- Others viewing them as their source instead of God.
- They could use their enthusiasm for giving to pressure others to give.
- Impulsive, frugal or stingy

These folks see life in terms of giving gifts. They love to share and distribute the wealth.

Biblical examples are Abraham, Solomon, Dorcas, and Luke.

The Motivational Gift of Administration

This gift might also be referred to as the gift of ruling or the gift of leadership. Those with this gift are excellent organizers, administrators, and leaders. They love to coordinate the efforts of others to reach a common goal. They are motivated to assist the body of believers reach their goals and achieve the fulfillment of their ministry. They have the vision to see long range and know how to break down a massive project into short term goals. They know how to delegate appropriate tasks to others and motivate them to complete the tasks.

They strive to maintain unity in those they are leading. They will not assume responsibility to lead a group without being given the authority to do so, unless there is no other leader available. They are able to withstand a great deal of pressure and even tolerate the criticism of others when necessary to see a task completed. Once a project is finished, they look for a new one to begin.

They prefer to leave smaller details to others; they have the ability to see ahead to the long-term results of the completed project. The person with the gift of administration will usually write down their goals and develop a plan of action to complete those goals.

They experience great satisfaction in seeing a project reach completion. They are positive in their leadership style and know how to encourage and motivate others to do their best. They expect loyalty from the people they lead. They set deadlines for themselves and work hard to complete the work within that deadline. They have a great deal of zeal to see a project through to completion, even in the midst of difficult circumstances.

What is the person with this gift vulnerable to?

- Pride, legalism, and control

- Insensitivity

- Lack of patience with others who are less able

- Insecurity

- Callous and uncaring

- Task focused instead of ministry focused

- Failure to get rest and stay healthy because of zeal to accomplish a task

- Their high standards make others feel driven instead of led.

- Critical of others who are less organized

- Their zeal can cause them to forge ahead of God and the Holy Spirit to start a project.

Biblical examples are Nehemiah, Moses, Joseph, and David.

The Motivational Gift of Mercy

Those with the gift of mercy are full of compassion, understanding, and empathy for others; sensitive, emotional, sympathetic, and merciful. They have the ability to feel what others are feeling (empathy) enabling them to minister to other's needs spiritually as well as emotionally. They have a deep-seated need to comfort others who are in distress, empathizing with them in their time of need.

People with this gift may overlook the shortcomings and quirks of others, giving mercy even when it may not be deserved. They tend to attract hurting people to themselves. Their primary concern is the emotional and spiritual needs of those they minister to rather than the physical and practical needs.

Because these are highly sensitive individuals, they are also easily hurt by others. Normally they avoid confrontation, but should they sense insincerity they can become bold and outspoken in order to protect those that are hurting.

They work well with others who possess this same gift. Repression of their feelings can lead to depression. They are excellent listeners and often make good counselors. They are very intuitive about things that can possibly hurt others. These people often develop friendships or relationships with the people who have the gift of prophecy. Perhaps the saying, "opposites attract" may apply here.

These sensitive people are vulnerable to:

- Depression

- Emotion

- Avoiding confrontation even when needed

- Bitterness

- Their empathy for someone of the opposite sex can cause their motives to be misunderstood.

- Their sincerity makes them seem friendly but close relationships can be difficult for them.

- May suppress their feelings to be accepted by others.

- Their desire to be wanted can cause them to enter into co-dependent relationships.

These people are very comforting and caring people. They are very people oriented. Biblical examples include: The Good Samaritan, Dorcas, and John (the apostle).

Conclusion

In this chapter, I have introduced some of the characteristics of each gift while presenting areas of potential vulnerability. Anyone can fall prey to the vulnerability trip. A right attitude and a close intimate relationship with the Lord help to insulate us from this danger.

We must stay in close contact with Him so that we can hear His voice and be sensitive to the leading of Holy Spirit. Failure to do so can cause us to fall into error and misuse of our gift. We are all vulnerable and we need each other, but most of all we need to allow Holy Spirit to lead and guide us.

When we minister to others using the motivational gift God gave us, we feel joy, satisfaction, and fulfillment. It also strengthens our brothers and sisters by meeting their needs; we minister to one another at the joints of relationship in the body of Christ.

The body needs you and your gift, in your proper place, functioning in the way God intended you to function. We need each other to be complete and whole. None of us are insignificant; we each have our own part to play as we come together to form the body of Christ.

Chapter Eight:

The Power to Kill, the Poison of Offence

Do not take the bait, <u>don't</u> bite the apple. One of my favorite childhood movies was the Disney hit, Snow White and the Seven Dwarfs. The beautiful and innocent Snow White had a wicked stepmother, the queen. The stepmother became so jealous of Snow White's beauty that she devised a plot to have her killed. I'm sure you remember the story. Instead of killing her, she was taken to a cottage to live with the seven dwarfs.

All was well and life was good in the cottage with seven dwarfs. That is, until the queen discovered that Snow White was not <u>really</u> dead. Her anger at being tricked became volatile. So, she came up with another plan and this time she would take care of it herself. She disguised herself and took Snow White a poisoned apple.

I remember sitting on the edge of my seat in the Ritz Theater, wanting to shout out to Snow White, "Don't do it! Don't take the bait! It's poisoned! "I wanted to stop her, but I could not.

The apple looked beautiful, like a delicious treat; but it was not as it appeared. It was all a cruel trick. But alas, she took the bait anyway. Her good intentions had come to naught and she bit into the apple. So, she promptly fell asleep; a sleep from which no one could awaken her. Well no one except of course, for her sweet prince. There was one appointed to save her from this dastardly deed.

It all sounds strangely familiar, does it not? Like the story of Eve in the garden of Eden. Jealousy provoked evil, deception, death, and a hero named Jesus. Yet today, the jealousy continues. We have an adversary that wishes to deceive and take us out. His name is Satan, and one of his poisons of choice is the poison of offense. If he can convince us that we have a right to be offended, it will poison our minds.

Once we partake, there is only one remedy. We must exchange our offense with the forgiveness once given to us. We overcome evil with good. We overcome hate with love.

A better solution is to simply not pick up offense in the first place. We do have a choice, but we must exercise the right to choose. If we recognize it for what it is, we do not need to pick it up. We can choose to walk away and leave it alone to die. We can choose to say, "not this time Satan! I am not taking your bait. I don't want your apple of offense. I choose to love and forgive." Allow God's love to heal your heart and rid your mind of the poison of offense. Let Satan know that you are on to his tricks and not taking his bait.

A key to developing healthy relationships with one another and strengthening our union as members of the body starts with respect, trust, humility, and love. Respect begins with respecting ourselves and valuing who God created us to be. This is often lost in unhealthy and codependent relationships.

Insecure individuals may use manipulation and demeaning be-haviors to gain control over others. This is especially true if they feel intimidated or threatened in the relationship. Remember, this does not need to be a real threat. People who are insecure may perceive danger where there is none. Fear of losing control drives them to mistreat and manipulate those closest to them.

Avoiding such dysfunctional relationships begins with under-standing who we are and respecting the value God has placed within us. When we place value on who we are, we guard ourselves from those who would mistreat or abuse us out of their own pain. That does not mean we must avoid hurting people altogether, it does mean that we must approach and relate to them with the proper boundaries in place.

We would not purchase a diamond ring then lay it down on a park bench out of sight while we play ball with a group of neighborhood kids. We would not do that because we value the worth of that ring and we want to protect it from harm. How much more must we value and respect ourselves?

A healthy boundary protects the treasure God has placed within us. This is similar to placing our money and gems in a lock box for safe keeping. We must protect what is important to us and to God.

We accomplish this in our relationships by simply drawing a line and letting people know how we expect to be treated. We guard that boundary diligently. This alerts others that we respect ourselves and they are expected to do likewise. The reverse is also true. We need to know the boundaries of those we are in relationship with and respect them.

Even Jesus demonstrated this concept in choosing the disciples He wanted near him. Some were closer than others. We can create varying degrees of boundaries dependent upon the people we wish to fellowship with most closely. It is also dependent upon the level of trust we have established with that individual. A choice few have earned the right to be very close, while others we must keep at an arm's length.

Jesus would escape the crowds and take the twelve away to rest. But there were three that were closer to Jesus than the other nine. Finally, one of the three was His closest disciple, described as the one Jesus loved. Such closeness comes with greater responsibility, as demonstrated by Jesus designating John to care for His mother Mary.

We will not be as close to some members of the body as we are to others. It is important to know who you are to be in relationship with, how intimate the relationship should be, and where to draw the boundaries. Proper boundaries are healthy for all involved.

People who are emotionally and spiritually immature may have difficulty with boundaries. It is however crucial that boundaries be established. Those in the body who are more mature need to lead by example, establishing and maintaining safe boundaries with all.

Those who are less mature may not understand the need for boundaries, however the lack there of makes them vulnerable to harm. We must teach the value of protecting what God has invested in their person.

When two or more people enter a relationship where both are immature and lack healthy personal boundaries, the potential for the development of a dysfunctional relationship exists. This is especially true if one or both lack a healthy personal respect for themselves.

An insecure, dominant person may have a need to control others. In an attempt to create peace, the less dominant person may exchange personal power for submission in hopes of appeasing the other person and maintaining the relationship. However, this is a vicious, unending cycle. It requires increasingly more submission resulting in increasingly more abusive activities unless someone stops the cycle.

One of them must stop the cycle by exiting the relationship or getting help. Know that if you know people in dysfunctional relationships, it is difficult to aid them. First, one of the people must acknowledge they have a problem. Second, one of them must desire help. Some people are content in continuing their role either as the victim, or the one in control.

There are varying degrees of dysfunction, and often there is mutual consent to live in that manner. If both people are happy, and none is suffering from harm, there is no need to interfere. There is a bit of dysfunction in most families. However, if you have a concern that a person may need intervention to prevent harm, consult a pastor, counselor, or law enforcement as is appropriate for the situation.

We often think of abuse as being a part of a family or marital relationship. However, dysfunction does not know such boundaries. Dysfunction and abuse may creep into any relationship between two individuals when proper boundaries are not secured.

How healthy are your boundaries? Do you look to God as your source? Are you growing strong and mature or are there areas that you could work on? Some questions you may ask yourself:

- Do you value the opinions of others more than you value who God says that you are?

- How dependent are you on the affirmations of others?

- Do you become angry when others disagree with you?

- Does criticism ruin your day? Your week?

- How confident are you when you enter a room of strangers?

- Are you willing to do whatever it takes to make others happy?

- Do you need to be in control of the activities of others?

- Do you feel a need to always be in charge?

- Are you afraid to speak your mind and be yourself with certain people?

- Do you have to walk on eggshells to avoid the angry outbursts of others?

If you have answered yes to any of these questions, it may be time to do some serious soul searching. Contact your pastor our counselor to see if further assistance is advised.

The result of developing a proper respect for ourselves and others makes trust possible. If I know that someone has my back and will not air my dirty laundry for the world to see, yes, we all have some dirty laundry somewhere, I am willing to make myself vulnerable and transparent to them. It is all about trust.

This kind of trust is something we earn in varying degrees. When we extend trust in areas where the relationship has not been proven, we put our own personal wellbeing and the relationship at risk. We must be wise about those with whom we are willing to share our most personal thoughts.

Have they proven that they value you in that same way? Can you trust them with the treasures hidden in you? Respect, trust, humility, and love; collectively we are talking about the development of right attitudes.

The scriptures regarding attitudes are numerous, but we will delve into just a few of them here. To start with in John 15:12 Jesus spoke,

> *"This is My commandment, that you love one another, just as I have loved you." Love one another... just as Jesus Christ loves you?*

We all know how difficult that can be to carry out at times, to love someone in spite of our differences. To love someone who has been unkind or cruel to you, but still... we must love.

Even when we do not have the love within ourselves, we can choose to love with the love of the Lord. Love is a choice, or it is the result of a decision that we make. God loves all of humanity and died for us while we were still sinners. We have the God of love on the inside, so we can choose to love with a God kind of love. That does not mean that we must tolerate abuse. Sometimes we must love from afar. Nevertheless, we have been commanded to love.

The Attitude of Christ

Jesus, using the little children that clamored about him as living examples, taught His disciples a valuable kingdom lesson. What type of attitude are we to have? Those who are greatest in the kingdom shall become like the little children and humble themselves....

At that time the disciples came to Jesus and said,

Who then is greatest in the kingdom of heaven?" [2]And He called a child to Himself and set him before them, [3]and said, "Truly I say to you, unless you are converted and become like children, you will not enter the kingdom of heaven. [4]"Whoever then humbles himself as this child, he is the greatest in the kingdom of heaven. [5]"And whoever receives one such child in My name receives Me; [6]but whoever causes one of these little ones who believe in Me to stumble, it would be better for him to have a heavy millstone hung around his neck, and to be drowned in the depth of the sea.

Paul also wrote of this kingdom principle in Philippians 2:5 saying this, *"Have this attitude in yourselves which was also in Christ Jesus."* What attitude? Let us back up two verses to gain a better understanding of what he is referring to here.

Do nothing from selfishness or empty conceit, but with humility of mind regard one another as more important than yourselves; [4]do not merely look out for your own personal interests, but also for the interests of others. Philippians 2:3-4

Paul was instructing us to have the attitude of humility. We are to look at others as being more important than ourselves. Jesus demonstrated this humble spirit throughout His life. The very act of laying down His own deity to become a man was the purest form of humility.

Then again, we have the act of laying down His life to die on the cross and taking our punishment for us or donning a towel to wash the feet of the disciples, and the examples go on. We are to be humble, we are to love, and we are to forgive our brothers and sisters.

The Forgiveness Factor

Then Peter came and said to Him,

"Lord, how often shall my brother sin against me and I forgive him? Up to seven times?" Jesus said to him, "I do

not say to you, up to seven times, but up to seventy times seven. Matthew 18:21-22

This is not to say that we are to continue to forgive when the sin against you is repeated and the sinner does not repent of his wrongdoing. This can be seen in Luke 17:3, "Be on your guard! If your brother sins, rebuke him; and if he repents, forgive him. The key here is the sincerity of the repentance. We are not to be a doormat for others to abuse.

The necessity of forgiveness of others was taught frequently during Jesus' ministry on the earth. He spoke of it in the Lord's Prayer; forgive others even as you have been forgiven. In Mark 11:25 He said, "And when you stand praying, if you hold anything against anyone, forgive them, so that your Father in heaven may forgive you your sins."

The examples cannot be exhausted, but the theme of forgiveness is ultimately the underlying theme of the whole bible. We have the free gift of forgiveness, not by works but by grace. Therefore, even as we have been given forgiveness, we are to give to others as well.

Conclusion

Wrong attitudes, unhealthy relationships, and immature believers can cripple or at the very least stunt the growth of the church. Offense can create poisoned mindsets. However, there is healing in the love of God for each man and each woman. There is hope that even in the most rag tag group of believers, health and wholeness is possible and necessary for the functioning of the body of Christ.

The church is a body of believers in varying states of maturity. Many come hurting, in pain, and in need of help. The church is much like a hospital for the sick and place of refuge for those searching for peace.

We reach out to those in need; we teach, we train, and we mentor those who are less mature. We maintain and grow in increasingly more healthy relationships with one another.

Healthy mature relationships equip the church so that we can become the empowered church, the body of Christ. The healthy empowered church bears fruit, and bearing fruit is the subject of our next chapter.

Chapter Nine:

The Power to Multiply

In the three years following Jesus's baptism by John the Baptist, there were many that followed Jesus. So many, He and His disciples would have to escape the crowds just to be alone. He would venture into the mountains or depart in a boat. Nevertheless, the people followed.

There were and still are, two types of people that choose to follow. First, there were those that followed out of curiosity or need. They were seeking healing, deliverance, or even food. Think of the times He fed the masses with a few fish and a couple loaves of bread. They followed Him for what He had to offer, or what He had in His hand or out of sheer curiosity alone. Jesus bore the fruit of forgiveness, healing, deliverance, and more.

This first group of people were fruit gatherers, for they gathered the fruit of Jesus' ministry. Many of us begin seeking Jesus in this very same manner. After all, we all have a need that only He can fill.

However, there is another group that followed Jesus, especially as outlined in the gospels. Let us refer to them as the fruit bearers. Jesus' twelve disciples fall into this second category.

While they may or may not have started following him out of need or curiosity, they quickly realized that Jesus had far more to offer in the form of relationship. Their relationship with Jesus grew strong and intimate. As a result, not only did Jesus change the world, so did all those who followed in His footsteps.

Think about it...when I was a child, we learned arithmetic one step at a time. First, we learned addition and subtraction. When we had successfully mastered the basic concepts, we went on to learn about multiplication and division. World changers understand the difference between addition and multiplication.

If you read about the growth of the church in the early days following Jesus' ascension, the book of Acts records that it grew by adding believers daily. Later in this same book, it talks about the believers being multiplied. Why would they start out adding and later multiplying? It was the gift of impartation.

Jesus imparted His life producing word into the lives of others and it bore fruit. However, He alone was only able to reach a small number of people. We know that He personally reached as many as would listen in the region of the world where He lived. There is no record of Him walking the streets of Singapore or Moscow. There was no television or computer, there were no trains, planes, or automobiles to transport Him to faraway places.

Jesus reached those He could reach on foot, those who were within listening range of His voice. Then He commissioned His followers to go and do the same. They were to impart what He had taught them into the lives of others, who in turn were to do the same.

The Word has the power to multiply and bear fruit in the lives of all that are willing to receive. It changes ordinary people into extraordinary people, people with the ability to be fruitful and multiply. Those who willingly accept their assignment, go on to reach and teach others and change the world. Believers who receive the Word for themselves, add to the church. Believers who receive and then share with others multiply the church.

From the young mother nursing her brand-new baby, to the missionary trekking through the jungles of deep dark Africa, we each have our assignment. Each assignment big or small is equally important to the kingdom as are we. If we each do our part and fulfill our assignment, we have the ability to change the world in which we live.

When the seeds of God's Word become embedded in the lives of believers, those seeds have the ability to take root, to grow, and mature. The maturated seed then bears fruit. We have each been impregnated with the seed of God's Word, and if allowed to mature, the Word will bear fruit.

Bearing Fruit

As vessels of honor, we are clothed and filled with the very glory of God. We possess His DNA in our spirit. We take off the old man and his nature and put on the new man becoming transformed by the Word.

> *And do not be conformed to this world, but be transformed by the renewing of your mind, so that you may prove what the will of God is, that which is good and acceptable and perfect. (Romans 12:2)*

We are to grow up into the fullness of the character and attributes of God himself. Jesus is the measuring stick guiding us to perfection by personal example. What a lofty goal! Nevertheless, we are to run our race and move toward the goal of perfection.

We are also light bearers, full of God's glory. This light, allowed to shine forth in the lives of believers, fills the whole earth with God's glory. Evidence of spiritual maturation and transformation is apparent in the manifested fruit we exhibit in our everyday lives, as seen here:

> *But the fruit of the Spirit is love, joy, peace, patience, kindness, goodness, faithfulness, gentleness, self-control; ... Galatians 5:22-23a*

Also, in Matthew it says:

> *You are the salt of the earth; but if the salt has become tasteless, how can it be made salty again? It is no longer good for anything, except to be thrown out and trampled underfoot by men.[14] "You are the light of the world. A city set on a hill cannot be hidden; [15] nor does anyone light a lamp and put it*

under a basket, but on the lampstand, and it gives light to all who are in the house.

[16] Let your light shine before men in such a way that they may see your good works and glorify your Father who is in heaven. Matthew 5:13-16

Fruit or Vegetable?

What is the difference between a fruit and a vegetable? Fruits differ from vegetables by the fact that fruits have seed bearing structures, they develop from the ovary of a flowering plant. Young flowering plants may have the potential to reproduce themselves and produce fruit, but that potential cannot be realized until the plant has grown to full maturity.

Vegetables on the other hand are harvested from all other parts of the plant. Vegetables may come from the root, leaves, or stem of the plant. Vegetables are considered annual plants and die off at the end of the growing season. Flowering plants and trees are considered perennials because they reproduce more year after year.

Fruits create seeds in the ovary of the plant. The seed is capable of becoming a mature plant, but it must first be planted, fed, watered and allowed to grow to full maturity. Only then does it fulfill its potential to bear fruit of its own. The first requirement for fruitfulness is maturity.

The Boastful Tree

One popular story about unfruitfulness is found in Mark 11:13. Jesus was hungry, and seeing a fig tree in full foliage, covered with leaves, He looked for its fruit but found none. Why did Jesus curse the fig tree in Mark 11:13?

It was not time for the fig tree to bear fruit. It was out of season! The leaves that typically grow after the fruit appears, were already on the tree. Therefore, a tree in full foliage should also be bearing fruit, but this fig tree was not.

When Jesus discovered the appearance of the leaves and realized it was _false_ evidence of fruitfulness, He cursed the tree. Not because it was not bearing fruit out of season, but because it was representing itself as being fruitful when it was not. It was a fake, an impostor. It was pretending to be something it was not.

This can be likened to the Jewish nation having an outer appearance of fruitfulness; they boasted of righteousness, but the evidence proved to be false. While man cannot look on another man's heart to judge his intent, man can look for evidence of his fruit. Fruit boasts of what the heart contains. You may try to disguise a tree as a pear tree, but when the apples begin to fall you will know the truth.

We know that there is a season for all things. There is a time to reap and a time to sow, a time to plant, and a time for harvest. There is a time to be born, and a time to die. There is a season in which we are expected to become mature and fruitful in the kingdom of God.

Unfortunately, some get stuck and fail to grow past infancy. No one wants to see a twenty-year old in diapers. Likewise, God expects us to grow to full spiritual maturity.

> _Ephesians 4:13 until we all attain to the unity of the faith, and of the knowledge of the Son of God, to a mature man, to the measure of the stature which belongs to the fullness of Christ._ [14] _As a result, we are no longer to be children, tossed here and there by waves and carried about by every wind of doctrine, by the trickery of men, by craftiness in deceitful scheming;_ [15] _but speaking the truth in love, we are to grow up in all aspects into Him who is the head, even Christ,_

God does not want us to remain in spiritual infancy. We are to grow up and mature, we are to become fruitful and multiply, in other words, reproduce. Spiritual maturity makes us fruit bearing.

As Christians, we need to plant ourselves on the foundation of our faith which is Jesus. We must feed on the Word daily and exercise our faith; for faith that is exercised grows. Finally, we need to maintain a healthy connection to our Father God through prayer.

Healthy Connections

Staying connected is the key. We need to be connected to one another and to God. Simply said, we need to grow in the Word, be diligent in prayer, and in developing healthy mature relationships with one another.

> *Hebrews 10:23-25 Let us hold fast the confession of our hope without wavering, for He who promised is faithful; and let us consider how to stimulate one another to love and good deeds, not forsaking our own assembling together, as is the habit of some, but encouraging one another; and all the more as you see the day drawing near.*

Let us not allow the enemy of our soul to separate us from the very ones with which we were meant to serve and fellowship. His end game is to divide and conquer, and ours must be to love and forgive. In unity we become fruitful, multiply, and fill the whole earth with God's glory. Unity is made possible through heathy mature relationships with one another and with God.

We cannot afford the luxury of remaining children, being tossed to and fro by every wind of doctrine. We must grow up into him who is the head. We must grow up into the fullness of the stature of Jesus Christ. Growing up, taking our place, and fulfilling our destiny... we can come together to change the world and establish God's kingdom. World changers unite... we have much to do. The world needs us.

> *For the anxious longing of the creation waits eagerly for the revealing of the sons of God. Romans 8:19*

Chapter Ten:

The Power for Success

Success, we all want it but how do we achieve it? The road to success is all too often laden with multiple setbacks and failures. The first example that comes to mind is Thomas Edison. We know that history tells us he failed some 1000 times before successfully creating our lightbulb.

Failure seemed to be his friend. Nevertheless, persistence in the face of failure helped him overcome. He eventually succeeded in achieving his dream. This is an important lesson for each of us today. Don't give up on the dream. In those moments when success seems so far away, we need to remember the story of Thomas Edison.

> *The thief comes only to steal and kill and destroy; I came that they may have life and have it abundantly. John 10:10*

The enemy would have you believe that success is unattainable, or impossible. He would have you think that it is better to just give up on God and your God given dream, but don't believe it. He wants to rob you of your hope, your joy, and your peace,

The enemy has no power to take away anything that belongs to us. God promised us peace and joy, power and authority, over all the power of the enemy. Do not be deceived by the enemy's lies. Adam and Eve were given dominion and authority over the earth, but they gave it away through their disobedience. They were deceived and lost their authority. Jesus regained that authority. He paid the debt that we could not pay. He paid it with his blood through His obedience and death on the cross. Ephesians 1:20-23 tells us this:

> *...which He brought about in Christ, when He raised Him from the dead and seated Him at His right hand in the*

heavenly places, ²¹far above all rule and authority and power and dominion, and every name that is named, not only in this age but also in the one to come. ²²And He put all things in subjection under His feet and gave Him as head over all things to the church, ²³which is His body, the fullness of Him who fills all in all.

What was relinquished through disobedience was regained through obedience. Jesus secured the power and authority, and now we are seated in heavenly places with him. That power He has now extended to each of us who have accepted Him as our Savior.

But of course, the enemy has not stopped being our enemy. The enemy would steal our peace. The enemy would rob us of our joy. The enemy would divide and conquer us so that he might split the church and render her useless. However, he will not succeed. Through our obedience and trust in God we can overcome, because Christ has overcome…and we are in Him and He in us. Moving forward, we must choose to exercise the power and authority given to us through Jesus.

I am sure that most of you have heard the story behind the writing of the song, *"It Is Well With My Soul"*. The hymnist, Horatio Spafford, had lost a son to pneumonia and his business to the Chicago fire. Later, he was determined to travel to Europe with his remaining family.

He placed his wife and four daughters on a ship, but at the last moment he was forced to stay behind to resolve a business problem. He promised to board another ship and follow them a few days later. Tragically, the first ship sank; his wife was the only member of his family to survive.

He boarded another ship and traveled the same course several days later. He found himself over the location where his four daughters had drowned when he penned the words to the hymn, *"All is well with my soul"*. How could anyone who had just suffered such incredible loss have the faith to pen those words? Only by the grace of God, by faith he believed that all was well with his soul.

The power to survive such a tragedy and find peace in one's soul, is only possible through an intimate relationship with our Heavenly Father. It is under the shadow of His wings, by abiding in His presence, that we can find peace in times of trouble.

When one believer is weak, others in the family of God can lend their support and strength; enabling the one that is hurt to traverse to the other side of the trouble. It is the work of the paraclete, the Holy Spirit, expressing His love and care through the prayers and actions of our brothers and sisters in the Lord. This is how we can find comfort and strength in difficult times.

Together we are better, together we are strong. This is precisely why the enemy tries so hard to drive a wedge into our relationships with one another and with God. Alone we are vulnerable, but together we are invincible. Persistence, faith, and love are keys to our success. Just one last thought; obedience is better than sacrifice.

You Are a World Changer

World changers, we must unite! The power for our success, the power to change the world and establish the kingdom, is found in our unity. We were created in families for this very purpose. We were created for relationship. God knew we would need each other.

A few years ago, I opened the cabinet below my kitchen sink to find that everything inside had become wet. I could not see the source of the water but knew that I had a problem. I called a plumber. The plumber told me that the faucet had gone bad, but so had the hose connecting it to the water line. What a mess!

Sometimes our relationships with one another, or even with God, can get messed up, leaky, ineffective and in need of repair. Therefore, it is important that we examine our own hearts. We need to make amends when we have hurt our brothers and sisters. Are we coming together in love and respect for one another in humility? Are we extending the same grace to our brothers and sisters that God extended to us?

Next, we need to check how we are doing in our personal relationship with the Lord. Are we taking time to study, pray, and worship? Are we spending time alone with Him, or has life become so complicated that we have forgotten? It is that time of intimacy that helps us grow and mature.

What does it mean to be a world changer? You may be thinking right now, who me? Are you talking about me? How can I change the world? Some days I struggle just trying to change the ink cartridge in my printer, or in keeping the faucet from leaking!

You and I are in good company. Many of the legendary bible heroes struggled with those same self-doubts. Take Moses, Gideon, Sarah, and what about Naomi and Ruth? We know they all suffered from doubt and struggled with fear, yet by the grace of God they persevered.

Don't Abort the Dream

Joseph had a dream and he tried to tell his family, but they did not believe him. His family discredited the report. Nevertheless, years later after much heartache and tribulation, the dream came to pass.

Samuel came to anoint the next king, and all of David's brothers were brought before him. No one thought David could be the chosen one, he was considered the least of these. David did not allow the opinions of others, including his family, to rob him of his God given destiny.

Moses was chosen and was spared death as an infant. He was raised in the household of Pharaoh, not as a Jew, but was adopted into an Egyptian family. He had it made, living the life of royalty! Nevertheless, Moses did not embrace the life of a prince. Rather, he held firm to his roots. As a result, many years later he became the deliverer of his nation.

None of these heroes allowed the opinions of others, or their circumstances to limit who they would become. They laid ahold of the dream of God for their life and did not let go until it came to pass. Wait for it. Wait for it. Wait for it! Prepare for it with all of your heart while you wait. Don't abort the dream of God for your life. <u>Wait</u> for the vision for it shall surely come to pass. See Habakkuk 2:2

What is Your Potential?

You are the called one of God. You are special, you are unique, you are one of a kind. When God created you, He packed you full of the potential to become. I call that your "spiritual DNA."

> *For I know the thoughts that I think toward you, saith the Lord, thoughts of peace and not of evil, to give you an expected end. Jeremiah 29:11*

> *According as He hath chosen us in Him before the foundation of the world, that we should be holy and without blame before Him in love. Ephesians 1:4*

Just because an individual may be gifted in areas that make them great candidates for medical school or law school, gifted musicians or artists, it does not mean they will utilize those gifts. It simply means the potential exists. We must each choose what to do with the potential we have been given.

God has a hidden seed of potential in each of us. *What will <u>you</u> do with the potential God gave you?* Think about it for a moment. We are full of EVERYTHING we could possibly need to become who we were created to be! We simply need to tap into that potential and develop it.

An Identity Formed in Christ

Too often we identify ourselves by what we do for a living or by the role that we play, in church or other social settings. We may see our self-worth as attached to that role or job, instead of in who God says that we are. It then becomes a performance-based identity rather than a God given birthright.

What do I mean by performance-based? Once we stop performing the activity or fulfilling the role... we cease to feel valuable; to our family, to society, to God, or the kingdom. That is a performance-based identity.

Our God given identity is not based upon our performance, but it is based upon God's intention when He created us. Even before He formed us in our mother's womb, He knew us, and He knew who He had created us to be!

Years ago, when my children were in high school, I managed our church's education department as well as fulfilling the role of youth pastor. Some things happened within the church body and the church eventually disbanded. I remember stepping out of my position there and beginning the task of finding another church.

I suddenly found myself wondering, who am I? I had mistakenly identified with the role that I played. My self-worth had been misplaced. The performance of activities related to that position had become my identity. Once I no longer performed those activities, I experienced anger, grief, and depression. I was having an identity crisis.

Our self-worth and identity must not be based on a role, a position, a title, or performance. We must learn to derive our personal self-worth from being a child of God. If we never do one thing for the Kingdom, we are still valuable in His sight, simply because of who he is. When we get that priority right, then we can go on to fulfill our call, and pursue our destiny in Him.

That being said, we honor our Heavenly Father by allowing His image to shine in us. Growing brighter and brighter each day. Not because of who we are, but because of who He is in us. The image of God is our spiritual DNA and we can choose to allow that image to develop and grow, transforming us; or we can choose to remain as spiritual children.

How can you change the world? Know who you are. Not who people say that you are, but who God says that you are. Know your gifts and talents; take the time to discover God's plan and purpose for your life. Take the time to develop a close intimate relationship with him.

Corporate Success

Thus far in this chapter, we have been discussing the success of the individual believer to fulfill their God given role. What we have not addressed is the success of the corporate body. How might we define success, and furthermore, how might the church achieve that success?

If you recall, the title of this book is, *"The Power of Unity."* We also have a subtitle, *it is "Empowered Believers Empower the Church"*. It is the role of the church to provide a place of refuge, peace, and comfort for the sick, the hurting and the lost. It is the role of the church to equip believers with the knowledge and wisdom they need to grow. It is to provide fellowship, education, and support.

God never intended for the church to be a spectator sport. The church is where God's administrative team, the five-fold ministry, prepares the believers to do the work of the ministry. Success is when the needs of the individual believers are met by the corporate body. When we each take responsibility for our own personal growth, developing healthy interpersonal relationships with God and with one another, we will be on the road to success.

Yes, we do need a governing body to keep order. We need a shepherd to protect and care for the sheep, but we also need to grow up and take our place. There is one body, but there are many members. We each have a role to play, we each have responsibilities to one another, and we are each needed.

No one else can do what you are called to do, quite like you. The church is where all hands must be on deck, working together in harmony and unity fulfilling the call of God upon the earth. Amen.

Conclusion:

The Power to Become

I do not ask on behalf of these alone, but for those also who believe in Me through their word; that they may all be one; even as You, Father, are in Me and I in You, that they also may be in Us, so that the world may believe that You sent Me.

The glory which You have given Me I have given to them, that they may be one, just as We are one; I in them and You in Me, that they may be perfected in unity, so that the world may know that You sent Me, and loved them, even as You have loved Me. John 17:20-23

Unity, a concept that seems impossible. However, it was Jesus' prayer, that we might be one even as they are one. The word "they" is a reference to God the Father, God the Son, and God the Holy Spirit; the three are different persons but united as one. We call the sum total of the three, the Trinity or the Godhead. Man was made in the image of God, in three parts. Man has a spirit and a soul, and they are housed in a body.

Likewise, Jesus prayed that the individual members of the church might collectively come together. Each member distinctly unique, but each one comes together in their proper place with the gifts and talents with which they have been endowed to form the body of Christ.

Together they are to have one heart, one mind, and one spirit. Spiritual children cannot, the potential is dormant and unachieved. Spiritually mature believers allow and participate as the Word of God transforms their hearts and their minds. It is in maturity, submission, and obedience that unity becomes possible.

Then Jesus said to His disciples, "If anyone wishes to come after Me, he must deny himself, and take up his cross and follow Me. Matthew 16:24

The cross is a place of submission and obedience to the Father. No longer viewing the world as what can it do for me, but rather what can I do to change the world?

The church is *"empowered to become"* when each one of us accepts the responsibility to become who we were called to be, to do what we are called to do, in the place we were called to do it. There is power in unity to become what the whole world is searching for; the power to become the body of Christ, the power to become the glorified bride.

We are better together, we are stronger together, we are powerful together! There is, *Power in Unity.*

Lord help us come together in unity as one, even as You are one. God grant us the ability and the desire to set aside our personal differences and our personal agendas in exchange for yours. Lord please reveal yourself in your children, the whole world awaits. Amen

There truly is power in unity! Change will not begin in the masses; it will begin in the one. Are you willing to do your part?

God Bless,

Dr. Kathy

Bibliography

Barnett Tommy Leadership/ Future Pastors [Online] Charisma Leader. - April 30, 2004 .- https://ministrytodaymag.com/leadership/finance/281-features/8958-future-pastor.

Eckhardt John God Still speaks [Book]. - Lake Mary, Florida: Charisma House, 2009.

Green Matthew Understanding the Fivefold Ministry [Book].- Lake Mary, Florida : Charisma House, 2005.

Smith Kathy J. Effective Pastoral Care Ministry in the Local Church [Book]. - Ramona, CA : Vision Publishing, 2016.

Smith Kathy J. Treasures of the Heart, The Gifts of the Trinity [Book]. - Ramona, CA : Vision Publishing, 2013.

About the Author

Dr. Kathy Smith has a Doctoral Degree in Leadership from Vision International University and an Associate Degree in Nursing from Excelsior College.

She is the Director of Communications and Publishing at Vision International University, and an ordained minister with the Assemblies of God International Fellowship.

Formerly from Ohio and North Carolina, she lived in Ramona, CA from 2012 to 2018. In 2018 she relocated to Grand Blanc, Michigan and continues to work for Vision International University.

As an author and educator, she travels to minister in local churches as the Lord leads. Her travels have taken her to the Dominican Republic, El Salvador, Austria, and Brazil. She has also been published in Christian magazines and publications and has appeared on Christian television and radio programs.

She has authored the books:

- *Treasures of the Heart, The Gifts of the Trinity,*

- *Wisdom Speaks: Hearing Her Voice In A Noisy World,*

- *Effective Pastoral Care Ministry in the Local Church*

- *Healthcare Chaplaincy*

- *The Power of Unity*

You may get more information on her website at: www.planpurposedestiny.org

If you are interested in scheduling her to speak, you may contact her at ksmith.vision.edu@gmail.com

www.ingramcontent.com/pod-product-compliance
Lightning Source LLC
LaVergne TN
LVHW021513080426
835509LV00018B/2503